Putting Corporate Parenting into Practice

A handbook for councillors

Di Hart and Alison Williams

NCB's vision is of a society in which children and young people contribute, are valued, and their rights respected. Our mission is to improve children and young people's experiences and life chances, reducing the impact of inequalities. NCB aims to:

- reduce inequalities of opportunity in childhood
- ensure children and young people can use their voice to improve their lives and the lives of those around them
- improve perceptions of children and young people
- enhance the health, learning, experiences and opportunities of children and young people
- encourage the building of positive and supportive relationships for children and young people with families, carers, friends and communities
- provide leadership through the use of evidence and research to improve policy and practice.

NCB has adopted and works within the UN Convention on the Rights of the Child.

Published by NCB
NCB, 8 Wakley Street, London EC1V 7QE
Tel: 020 7843 6000
Website: www.ncb.org.uk

Registered charity number: 258825

NCB works in partnership with Children in Scotland (www.childreninscotland.org.uk) and Children in Wales (www.childreninwales.org.uk).

Second edition
ISBN: 978 1 907969 96 6

British Library Cataloguing in Publication Data
A catalogue record for this book is available from the British Library

Typeset by Saxon Graphics Ltd, Derby
Printed by Hobbs the Printers Ltd, Totton, Hampshire

Contents

Foreword

Children in care need sustained support and active encouragement to reach their full potential. I know from personal experience that the results can be dramatic, but many children in care and care leavers still underachieve. The role of corporate parents in helping all children and young people in care to hit the heights we all aspire for our own children is crucial. It is your responsibility as their corporate parents to ensure that those talents are helped to develop and grow. You can open up new opportunities for children, enable them to live as rewarding lives as possible and empower them to make choices over their own lives.

Part of the problem has been the continuing low aspirations and expectations for children in care. This is changing, but not nearly fast enough. With the right support children in care can and do achieve a great deal. Valuing and supporting the education of children in care is one of the most important contributions a corporate parent can make to their lives. It is about investing in their future.

Children in care need to be a priority across the whole council, not just for children's services. Sport, culture and leisure have major contributions to make in improving the life chances of children in care. Participation in the arts or sport can transform children's lives by improving self-esteem, encouraging social interaction and widening horizons. If a child is musical, encourage them to learn an instrument and give them the support they need to do this. Some councils provide discount schemes at local leisure centres, others use community arts projects to help these children gain confidence and skills. The rule of thumb should be to give children in care the same opportunities as you would give your own children.

The key to supporting children in care effectively is listening and acting on their views. They know better than anyone else what works well, what is less successful, and what needs to change. Every local authority has a Children in Care Council (CICC) and regular meetings between them and senior members of the authority, as their corporate parents, is essential.

I know that many of you came into politics, like me, to help the most vulnerable in our society, to help change your communities for the better. You have no greater responsibility than when you are acting as corporate parents. It is only through good quality care and support that children in care stand a chance of beginning their adult life with a real prospect of success. I am sure this is what you also aspire to and hope that this guide will help you achieve it.

EDWARD TIMPSON
Children's Minister

Introduction

The coalition government has stated that improving the lives of children in care is a national priority. This is because, in spite of considerable attention over recent years, there continues to be a gap between their outcomes and those of their peers, with significantly worse educational achievements, more likelihood of being convicted of an offence and more likelihood of becoming homeless. They may also be at risk of further abuse while in care and a number of inquiries have highlighted what can go wrong.[1, 2, 3] This risk is increased where children are placed out of the authority, are disabled or do not have access to independent people.

However, there is more to being a good parent than keeping children safe. Every child needs to feel that parents are 'there' for them, including children in the care system.

> *Social workers, I had so many ... Half of the social workers I didn't know. They used to change like that ... I never even knew I had a new social worker and I was trying to ... tell her everything about my life.*
>
> (17-year-old girl in care)[4]

Corporate parents want to do a good job. The complication for children in care is that those responsible are the elected members and officers of the local authority. These materials are designed to support corporate parents in this important task and are updated versions of *Putting Corporate Parenting into Practice*.[5] Their focus is on the leadership and commitment that only members and senior officers can provide, rather than front-line staff and carers working directly with the children themselves. The emphasis is on practical tools and training materials, not guidance, and these are presented at different levels of complexity in recognition of the fact that responsibilities differ according to an individual's specific role.

Why is corporate parenting important?

The reasons for children needing to be looked after, such as parental abuse, neglect or abandonment, will have already placed them at a disadvantage. It is essential that their experiences in public care compensate for this disadvantage rather than compound it. Their

---

1   Utting, W (1997) *People Like Us: The Report of the Review of the Safeguards for Children Living Away From Home*. London: Department of Health and Welsh Office.

2   Waterhouse, R, Clough, M and Le Flemming, M (2000) *Lost in Care: Report of the Tribunal of Inquiry into the Abuse of Children in Care in the Former County Council Areas of Gwynedd and Clwyd Since 1974*. Norwich: The Stationery Office.

3   Office of the Children's Commissioner for England (2012) *Briefing for the Rt Hon Michael Gove MP, Secretary of State for Education, on the Emerging Findings of the Office of the Children's Commissioner's Inquiry into Child Sexual Exploitation in Gangs and Groups, with a Special Focus on Children in Care*. Available at: http://www.childrenscommissioner.gov.uk/content/publications/content_580 (accessed 14 January 2013).

4   Quoted in Blades, R, Hart, D, Lea, J and Willmott, N (2011) *Care: A Stepping Stone to Custody?* London: Prison Reform Trust.

5   Hart, D and Williams, A (2008) *Putting Corporate Parenting into Practice: Developing an Effective Approach*. London: National Children's Bureau.

corporate parents should be their champions in the fight to get them what they need – and to make sure they are safe.

The most important benefit of effective corporate parenting will be to improve the outcomes for individual children, but there are other benefits. If suitable services have been developed that match the needs of the children being looked after, there will be less need to look outside the authority in order to purchase emergency or specialist provision. Such provision is not only costly but is less likely to provide the child with stability over time, leading to worse outcomes.[6] If children are not provided with good care at an early stage, they are at risk of entering a downward spiral of disrupted placements, higher costs and increasingly complex needs.

A final consideration is the impact that effective corporate parenting will have on the local authority's performance. Although the government no longer sets targets for local authority services, the expectation is that they should monitor their own performance in a number of key areas, such as whether children have been receiving regular health assessments, have achieved satisfactory educational attainments or are living in stable placements. Ofsted will in future examine not only local authority services for looked after children but the effectiveness of an authority's corporate parenting arrangements.

In short, good local services and placements are likely to improve looked after children's life chances, be better value for money *and* contribute to good performance ratings.

Introducing the resource materials

The materials within this handbook are designed to help individual councillors to become effective corporate parents.

They are divided into the following sections:

- *Understanding the corporate parenting role.* A summary of the legal and policy context and description of different levels of responsibility.
- *A model of effective corporate parenting.* The components that need to be in place in order for a council to be effective corporate parents, including governance arrangements.
- *Working with children and young people.* A summary of key messages from looked after children and ideas about working in partnership with them.
- *Is the service good enough?* Materials to support corporate parents in assessing how well their own council is doing, using both quantitative and qualitative sources of information.
- *If you want know more....* Briefings on key topics relevant for corporate parents, where to look for examples of local practice, references and further sources of information.

---

6   Ward, H, Soper, J, Holmes, L and Olsen, R (2004) *Looked After Children: Counting the Costs – Report on the Costs and Consequences of Different Types of Child Care Provision Study* (CCFR Evidence 7). Loughborough University: Centre for Child and Family Research.

Understanding the corporate parenting role

Time and again, it is local councils, local leaders and local staff proving that children in care can and do succeed when the right people, systems and attitudes are in place.

(Edward Timpson, Children's Minister)[7]

This section explores the corporate parenting role in more detail. It includes:

- frequently asked questions
- a summary of the legal and policy context
- a description of the roles and responsibilities of specific members and officers
- a checklist of three different levels of responsibility within the council
- three activities for raising awareness among corporate parents.

Corporate parenting is not new – local authorities have always provided alternative care for children who, for whatever reason, cannot live at home. The responsibility of elected members was not always at the forefront, however. In 1998 the then Secretary of State for Health, Frank Dobson, wrote to councillors reminding them that they were ultimately accountable for the quality of care provided by their local authority and spelling out their specific responsibility to lead this work and to monitor its effectiveness.

This responsibility has become known as 'corporate parenting' in recognition that the task must be shared by the council as a whole. It is about more than providing food and shelter: a good corporate parent offers at least the same standard of care as would a reasonable parent. This means that looked after children should be cared about, not just cared for, and that *all* aspects of their development should be nurtured, requiring a 'corporate' approach from a range of council departments and partner agencies.

Developing a strategic approach to corporate parenting

Although the corporate parenting role is shared, front-line staff and carers working directly with children can only do a good job if there is effective leadership. In Ofsted's inspection programme of local authority safeguarding and looked after children's services, weak leadership and strategic planning were often associated with a poor service to children. For example:

'Too many local authorities inspected this year ... lacked a robust strategy for corporate parenting.'[8]

And this statement from an individual inspection suggests what was missing in one authority:

'A clearer articulation of the leadership, ambition and objectives for looked after children is yet to be provided for practitioners .... '

---

7   25 October 2012: *Speech to the National Adult and Children's Services Conference*. Available at: http://www. education.gov.uk/inthenews/speeches/a00216171/raising-our-ambitions-for-children-in-care

8   Ofsted (2011) *The Annual Report of Her Majesty's Chief Inspector of Education, Children's Services and Skills 2010/11: Children's Social Care*. Available at: www.ofsted.gov.uk/resources/annualreport1011 (accessed 14 January 2013).

After working with a number of authorities as part of the *Putting Corporate Parenting into Practice* project, we have concluded that this strategic direction is easiest to achieve when there is a single body within the council structure that has overarching responsibility. The components of this approach are described in the section entitled 'A Model of Effective Corporate Parenting'.

A focus on outcomes

Whatever the model adopted, for services to be effective they should be based on a needs analysis, followed by a decision about desired outcomes. The services most likely to achieve these outcomes can then be commissioned. Finally, there should be a process of review to establish if the services have resulted in the desired outcomes and to inform the next commissioning round. This cycle is illustrated in Figure 1.

Figure 1: Outcome-based analysis

The Every Child Matters programme initiated in 2004 defined the outcomes that children's services should be judged by as follows:

- be healthy
- stay safe
- enjoy and achieve
- make a positive contribution
- achieve economic well-being.

Although the programme is no longer government policy, the outcomes themselves are still useful. In terms of corporate parenting, there are particular obstacles that may prevent looked after children from achieving them. For example, some residential settings may be targeted by adults who are looking for children vulnerable to sexual exploitation or schools may be reluctant to accept children with a disrupted educational history. Corporate parents must ensure that they have an accurate picture of what their looked after children need in order to achieve good outcomes and then plan and commission services to match those needs. This will always require a partnership between agencies and departments, as children's services authorities will be unable to provide all the services that children require. Each council should ensure that local strategic plans, such as the Health and Well-being Plan, include a specific element on looked after children and care-leavers based on the expressed commitment of all agencies and council departments.

A 'good' corporate parenting strategy is not just a series of aspirational statements, although aspirations are important. The strategy sets out exactly how this vision will be achieved, by whom and when, and how corporate parents will know when they have achieved their objectives.

Frequently asked questions

Looking after children is never easy and looking after other people's children is even more challenging. Councillors have told us that they take the responsibility seriously but struggle to know how to translate it into practice. The following are examples of frequently asked questions.

1. Should councillors be taking an interest in the well-being of specific looked after children and advocating on their behalf?

The term 'corporate parent' implies a personal relationship and it is understandable that councillors would like to know more about the individual children cared for by their council. Looked after children sometimes lack inhibition about disclosing information and councillors should avoid asking questions about a child's personal history or family circumstances. It is not your role as a corporate parent to develop personal relationships with children but there may be other, more indirect, ways of following their progress. For example, you could receive regular updates about the educational progress or placement moves of a group of children so that you could act as their 'champion' in making sure they get what they need.

2. As a member of the corporate parenting group, can I rely on officers to tell us how well the children are doing?

It is crucial for councillors and officers to have a good working relationship based on mutual trust. Officers should give an honest portrayal of the service, including any weaknesses. Corporate parents have an individual responsibility, however, and should base their judgements about the quality of care provided by their council on a number of different sources and not just reports from officers. Relevant sources include performance data, analyses of complaints and, importantly, the views of looked after children themselves.

3. How do I make sense of the data on the educational or other achievements of looked after children?

Most corporate parents will receive performance data on their council's service to looked after children, such as their attainment at school. This can be difficult to evaluate unless it is accompanied by some comparison with both past performance and data from comparable councils. This will demonstrate whether performance is improving and whether it is significantly better or worse than elsewhere. Statistics alone are never enough, however, and need to be accompanied by an explanation of the story behind them. For example, a decline in the number of babies coming into care could be an indication of a successful local Sure Start programme *or* a failure of a local authority's child protection service to identify children at risk of harm at an early stage.

4. As a lead member for children's services, how do I identify areas of the service that need to improve?

Lead members for children's services will need to have a close working relationship with their Director of Children's Services and should expect regular updates on the strengths and weaknesses of the service to looked after children. This can change quickly and it is not enough to rely on annual performance data. There will also be people 'closer to the ground' who will have ideas about areas for improvement, including the Children in Care Council and the Independent Reviewing Service. A good way of accessing this information is through a corporate parenting group, where reports on specific topics can be requested or key people invited to do a presentation. It is important not only to determine priorities but to agree the action that will be taken and to monitor its implementation.

5. Are other councils doing a better or worse job?

The performance data published annually by the Department for Education will allow you to make comparisons but there are other ways of finding out. For example, you could invite an authority to make a presentation to your corporate parenting group or set up a peer review process. Similar arrangements could be established with your Children in Care Council so that ideas are exchanged across authorities. There are also a number of websites that describe initiatives being taken by other authorities that will give you some ideas. For example, Ofsted publishes its inspection reports online,[9] the Centre for Excellence and Outcomes in Children and Young People's Services (C4EO) posts examples of validated or promising practice[10] and the Centre for Public Scrutiny publishes examples of thematic reviews undertaken by local scrutiny committees.[11]

6. What is the best way for corporate parents to work with the Children in Care Council?

There is no single model for how this should be done. Some councils invite their Children in Care Council to participate in their corporate parenting group, while others receive reports mediated by their participation service. It is essential that a local mechanism is established that works for both parties, otherwise there is a risk that the corporate parenting group and the Children in Care Council will operate in parallel rather than collaboratively. Joint activities, such as reviewing the local Care Pledge, may give a focus to the work. The first step is to ask the Children in Care Council what they would like to happen and to agree terms of reference for the working arrangements.

---

9   http://www.ofsted.gov.uk/children-and-families-services/for-childrens-social-care-providers-and-commissioners/find-children-a

10 http://www.c4eo.org.uk/themes/vulnerablechildren/localpractice.aspx?themeid=3

11 http://www.cfps.org.uk/library

7. As a lead member for children, how can I get all elected members to be active corporate parents?

This is a challenge, particularly in two-tier authorities. Councillors who are not part of the corporate parenting group may feel that they can leave responsibility to others. Ways of improving engagement are:

- to have induction/refresher training to raise awareness of the role among elected members
- to require all committee reports to consider and record the impact of decisions on looked after children
- to ask all elected members to make a pledge about their own contribution to promoting the welfare of the council's looked after children, such as attending celebration events or offering work experience placements
- to share the achievements and views of looked after children at meetings of the full council.

8. Where can I go for support on corporate parenting?

NCB has created a website to support corporate parents which is available at www.ncb.org.uk/corporateparenting and can also offer tailored training and consultancy to local authorities.

Legal and policy context

Legislative framework

The **Children Act 1989** is the primary legislation setting out local authority responsibility to children 'in need', including looked after children. Section 22 imposes a duty on local authorities to safeguard and promote the welfare of each child they look after. The **Children (Leaving Care) Act 2000** extended the responsibility of the local authority to young people leaving care, requiring them to plan the young person's transition to adulthood and provide ongoing advice and assistance until at least the age of 21.

The **Adoption and Children Act 2002** required all local authorities to appoint Independent Reviewing Officers (IROs) to review the care plans of looked after children, and the Act introduced Special Guardianship orders that provide permanence for children but are alternatives to adoption.

Local authorities have been entitled to expect other agencies to assist them in discharging their functions since the implementation of the Children Act 1989 (Section 27) but this was not a statutory responsibility until the **Children Act 2004**. This Act introduced a duty on named agencies both to cooperate with the local authority (Section 10) and to ensure that they take account of the need to safeguard and promote the welfare of children in fulfilling their own functions (Section 11). It also made provision for local authority areas to set up Children's Trusts, bringing together relevant agencies, and to develop a Children and Young People's Plan. These are not mandatory but can provide a mechanism for bringing relevant agencies and plans together so that children's needs are not lost.

The **Local Government and Public Involvement in Health Act 2007** placed a duty on upper-tier local authorities and primary care trusts to undertake a joint strategic needs assessment (JSNA) of their local population.

The **Children and Young Persons Act 2008** requires local authorities to take steps to secure sufficient suitable accommodation for looked after children within their area that meets their needs. It also strengthens the care planning process and the role of the Independent Reviewing Officer in monitoring the plan, and children's health and education plans are essential components of this.

The **Health and Social Care Act 2012** abolishes primary care trusts and will transfer responsibility for commissioning local health services, apart from primary care, to a Clinical Commissioning Group consisting of GP consortia. Primary care and specialist services will be commissioned by the NHS Commissioning Board, who will also be responsible for holding the Clinical Commissioning Groups to account. The Act also established Health and Well-being Boards, led by the Director of Public Health within the local authority, to improve the health and well-being of the local population and reduce health inequalities. Section 12 creates a new duty for local authorities to take steps to improve the health of people in their area.

The **Legal Aid, Sentencing and Punishment of Offenders Act 2012** has introduced a single remand order for children and young people under the age of 18 who are refused bail, which will mean that they become looked after children for the duration of the remand, and may mean that they are entitled to leaving care services.

Statutory guidance

The legislative framework is supported by statutory guidance that describes roles and responsibilities in more detail. Statutory guidance is more than just suggestions about good practice: it should be adhered to.

Who Pays? Establishing the Responsible Commissioner[12] determined that, for looked after children and care-leavers placed outside their home primary care trust (PCT) area, the 'originating' PCT is the 'responsible commissioner', even if the child has changed GP, and should make arrangements for the child's health assessments to be undertaken and for the provision of secondary health services. This will remain the case through any subsequent moves, although the commissioner can negotiate for agencies local to the placement to provide services on their behalf. Once Clinical Commissioning Groups consortia are in place, they will take the place of PCTs.

Statutory Guidance on Promoting the Health and Well-being of Looked After Children[13] placed the contribution of NHS agencies towards meeting the needs of looked after children on a statutory footing for the first time. The role of the PCT was to analyse the health needs of looked after children, plan and commission services, and monitor and review their effectiveness. Strategic Health Authorities were expected to monitor the performance of PCTs and to play a developmental and supportive role. Although PCTs have been replaced by Clinical Commissioning Groups, the government's 'mandate' to the NHS Commissioning Board for 2013–2015[14] says:

> 'We expect to see the NHS, working together with schools and children's social services, supporting and safeguarding vulnerable, looked-after and adopted children, through a more joined-up approach to addressing their needs.'

Promoting the Educational Achievement of Looked After Children: Statutory Guidance for Local Authorities[15] clarified the duty to actively support looked after children's education. Measures include the priority that must be given to looked after children in terms of school admission, restriction on the use of school exclusion and the introduction of personal education allowances to purchase tailored support.

The **Children Act 1989 Guidance and Regulations Volume 2: Care Planning, Placement and Case Review Regulations and Guidance**[16] clarify the expectations of care planning and review for looked after children and strengthen the role of the Independent Reviewing Officer (IRO) to challenge when identified needs are not being met. The manager of the service is required to prepare an annual report that should be made available to corporate parents.

The **Children Act 1989 Guidance and Regulations Volume 3: Planning Transitions to Adulthood for Care Leavers**[17] gives details of how care-leavers should be provided with comprehensive personal support so that they achieve their potential as they make their transition to adulthood. It

---

12   Department of Health (2007) *Who Pays? Establishing the Responsible Commissioner.* Available at: http://
      www.dh.gov.uk/en/Publicationsandstatistics/Publications/PublicationsPolicyAndGuidance/DH_078466
      (accessed 14 January 2013) and Commissioning Support Programme (2010) www.commissioningsupport.org.
      uk (accessed 14 January 2013).

13   Department for Children, Schools and Families (2009) *Statutory Guidance on Promoting the Health and
      Well-being of Looked After Children.* Available at: https://www.education.gov.uk/publications/standard/
      Healthanddisabilities/Page1/DCSF-01071-2009 (accessed 14 January 2013).

14   Department of Health (2012) *The Mandate: A Mandate from the Government to the NHS Commissioning
      Board – April 2013 to March 2015.* Available at: https://www.wp.dh.gov.uk/publications/files/2012/11/
      mandate.pdf (accessed 14 January 2013).

15   Department for Children, Schools and Families (2010) *Promoting the Educational Achievement of Looked
      After Children: Statutory Guidance for Local Authorities.* Available at: https://www.education.gov.uk/
      publications/standard/publicationDetail/Page1/DCSF-00342-2010 (accessed 14 January 2013).

16   Department for Children, Schools and Families (2010) *The Children Act 1989 Guidance and Regulations
      Volume 2: Care Planning, Placement and Case Review.* Available at: https://www.education.gov.uk/
      publications/standard/Lookedafterchildren/Page1/DCSF-00185-2010 (accessed 14 January 2013).

17   Department for Children, Schools and Families (2010) *The Children Act 1989 Guidance and Regulations
      Volume 3: Planning Transition to Adulthood for Care Leavers.* Available at: https://www.education.gov.uk/
      publications/standard/Lookedafterchildren/Page1/DFE-00554-2010 (accessed 14 January 2013).

includes the need for care-leavers to be living in suitable accommodation and receiving support to continue in education or training and to find employment.

Statutory Guidance: Securing Sufficient Accommodation for Looked After Children[18] requires local authorities to develop a plan to secure sufficient accommodation for looked after children within their local authority area and which meets their needs. They can only do this if they work in partnership with other agencies as the requirement is not just about accommodation and placements but also securing a 'diverse range of universal, targeted and specialist services working together to meet children's needs' and applies not only to looked after children but also those on the edge of care and at risk of custody.

Statutory Guidance on the Roles and Responsibilities of the Director of Children's Services and the Lead Member for Children's Services.[19] These roles are statutory and cover both the social care and education services of the local authority. These individuals should provide strong leadership and ensure that there is a clear line of accountability for children's well-being. They have particular responsibility for vulnerable groups of children, including those for whom they are corporate parents. The Lead Member should provide *political* leadership whilst the Director of Children's Services should provide *professional* leadership.

---

18   Department for Children, Schools and Families (2010) *Sufficiency. Statutory Guidance: Securing Sufficient Accommodation for Looked after Children.* http://media.education.gov.uk/assets/files/pdf/s/statutory%20 guidance%20securing%20sufficient%20accommodation%20for%20looked%20after%20children%20 march%202010.pdf
19   Department for Education (2012) *Statutory Guidance on the Roles and Responsibilities of the Director of Children's Services and the Lead Member for Children's Services.* Available at: https://www.education.gov.uk/ publications/standard/Childrenandfamilies/Page1/DFE-00034-2012 (accessed 14 January 2013).

Roles and responsibilities

All councillors and council officers share corporate parenting responsibility and cannot abdicate this responsibility in favour of those they see as being more central, but this does not mean that everyone has the same role. Clearly those councillors who chair corporate parenting groups, or who are involved with thematic scrutiny of children's services, will have a greater role day-to-day than those who are responsible for environmental or planning decisions. Even the Planning Committee, however, will be making decisions that affect looked after children, such as deciding whether to approve an application to open a new children's home.

Similarly, officers will have differing roles. The Director of Children's Services will be pivotal in ensuring that systems and services are in place to meet the needs of looked after children, but the Director of Housing will need to ensure that there is a range of high quality housing options available for children when they leave care, headteachers have a role in actively promoting their educational attainment and the Director of Public Health should make sure they are supported to live a healthy lifestyle.

Responsibility does not rest solely with top-tier authorities. Within county councils, district councillors may not have direct contact with the social work service but will be involved, for example, in making sure that their communities have adequate leisure facilities or public transport. As corporate parents, they should be considering whether these are accessible to looked after children and their carers.

Finally, responsibility extends beyond local authority services. So the new Clinical Commissioning Groups and health providers should actively promote the health of looked after children, while crime and disorder reduction partnerships and the new Police and Crime Commissioners will need to consider whether looked after children are being supported in avoiding offending behaviour.

In reality, the range of potential partners in meeting the needs of looked after children is as wide as the number of agencies and organisations within the area. Councillors often have multiple roles within their locality, such as school governors. The duty to be an effective corporate parent is paramount, and councillors must consider and promote the welfare of looked after children and care-leavers throughout these various activities. For example, a school governor should advocate that a looked after child be welcomed into the school that will best meet their needs. They will act as a champion for the child in challenging the prejudice that looked after children have a negative effect on the attainment targets of the school or inevitably have behavioural problems. This is what a reasonable parent would do.

Calderdale Council has produced specific advice for councillors who serve as school governors in respect of the corporate parenting role for looked after children.

Key structures/posts

- **Lead Member for Children's Services.** This individual has *political* responsibility for the leadership, strategy and effectiveness of local authority children's services.
- **Director of Children's Services.** This person has *professional* responsibility for the leadership, strategy and effectiveness of local authority children's services.
- **Independent Reviewing Officers.** IROs are responsible for reviewing and monitoring each looked after child's case and care plan and challenging poor practice. They must be qualified social workers and independent from the line management of the child's case.
- **Social workers.** Each looked after child must have a qualified social worker allocated to them, responsible for developing and implementing their care plan.

- **Residential and foster carers.** Each looked after child should be provided with a placement to live in that is best able to keep them safe and meet their needs. This can be with foster carers, in residential care or a more specialist setting if their needs are complex.
- **Kinship carers.** Some looked after children are placed with family or friends, sometimes known as 'kinship carers'.
- **Adopters.** Where it is decided that a child cannot be cared for by their own family, it is important that a permanent alternative home is provided. This may be through adoption, where the adoptive family acquires full parental responsibility and the child ceases to be looked after once an adoption order is made.
- **Special guardians.** Where a child has significant ties with someone other than a parent who is looking after them, such as a relative or foster carer, that person can be given parental responsibility through a special guardianship order. This means that they will bring the child up, and the child is no longer looked after, but the child is not part of their family in the same way as an adopted child.
- **Independent visitors.** Every looked after child is entitled to have an independent visitor – an adult completely outside the care system who can befriend them. This is especially useful for children who have little or no contact with their family.
- **Advocates.** An advocate has a more specific role than that of an independent visitor, in that they support the child's participation in decision making and make sure that their voice is heard. They may accompany children to review meetings if the child requests it.
- **Mentors.** A mentor is more likely to work with older children or care-leavers. Their role is to establish a positive relationship that will motivate achievement in education, training and employment by building the young person's confidence.
- **Personal advisors.** Young people entitled to services as a care-leaver must be allocated a personal advisor to act as a focal point for planning their transition to adulthood. The role is not the same as that of a social worker and personal advisors will continue to offer support after the young person has left care.
- **Children in Care Council.** Local authorities are required to establish a Children in Care Council to represent the views of looked after children to those responsible for the service.
- **Participation workers.** Many local authorities have created specific posts, or contracted local voluntary sector partners, to support children's participation in the Children in Care Council or to seek their views in other ways.
- **Corporate parenting group/board.** Although not a statutory requirement, most local authorities have established a group of elected members to oversee the corporate parenting function of the local authority.
- **Children's Trusts.** These are partnership arrangements bringing together children's services within a local authority area. They are no longer mandatory but, if not established, alternative mechanisms to work in partnership need to be in place.
- **Health and well-being boards.** A forum for key leaders from the health and social care system to work together to improve the health and well-being of the local population and reduce health inequalities. As a group at risk of poor health, it will be important to ensure that the needs of looked after children and care-leavers form part of their remit. It will also be important to clarify links with the Children's Trust or other bodies responsible for children's services.
- **Virtual school head.** Although not yet mandatory (the Children and Families Bill may change that), it is good practice for local authorities to have a virtual school head or equivalent to collate information about the attainment of looked after children as if they were in a single school, and to provide challenge and support to help them make progress.
- **Designated teachers.** Every maintained school is required to appoint a designated teacher to promote the educational achievement of looked after children.
- **Designated doctors and nurses for looked after children.** These individuals have a strategic role that is separate from the direct service they may offer to individual children. Different local areas operate different models but it is important that, whichever model is used, arrangements are in place to enable the designated professionals to have an impact on the commissioning of health services for looked after children.

- **Child and adolescent mental health services (CAMHS).** Dedicated provision is required for looked after children. In some authorities this has led to the creation of specialist teams; in others it has been interpreted more narrowly.
- **The PCT (to be replaced by Clinical Commissioning Groups).** These bodies and the local authority should agree joint action on the health needs of looked after children in their area and develop a joint commissioning strategy.
- **The Children and Young People's Plan (CYPP).** This is not mandatory but can serve to describe the aspirations for all children in an area. If the local authority has such a plan, it is useful to ensure that looked after children are identified as a group requiring specific services.
- **Joint Strategic Needs Assessment.** The JSNA is the process for identifying the current and future health and well-being needs of a local population, leading to agreed commissioning priorities that will improve outcomes and reduce health inequalities.
- **Director of Public Health.** The Director should be examining the health outcomes of looked after children to ensure that steps are taken to reduce inequalities.

A checklist of levels of responsibility within the local authority

The different levels of responsibility can be summarised as:

- universal responsibility (level 1)
- targeted responsibility (level 2)
- specialist responsibility (level 3).

Universal responsibility (level 1) checklist

Everyone who is elected to serve on, or is employed by, a council shares a collective responsibility towards the children the council looks after. This responsibility does not end when children leave care to live independently: the council must continue to provide support to care-leavers. The first step in fulfilling these responsibilities is to understand more about looked after children in general, then to consider the children looked after by *this* council, and finally to establish the individual contribution that each councillor must make. *All* councillors must ask themselves:

Do I understand why children need to be looked after, and the legal and policy framework that governs this?	
Am I aware of the governance arrangements for corporate parenting within my council?	
Do I know about the profile of the children looked after by the council – and the outcomes they are achieving compared with other local children?	
Can I be sure that we are providing the best care possible for our looked after children and care-leavers? Would it be good enough for my child?	
Am I aware of our local Care Pledge to looked after children and how I can contribute towards fulfilling it?	
Does the council have a corporate parenting strategy and, if so, what are the key points?	
Am I taking responsibility for promoting the welfare of looked after children and care-leavers in all my work for the council – and in my other capacities?	
Are there any celebration or other events that I can attend in order to demonstrate directly to looked after children that I want them to do well?	
Do I know what the most important issues are for our looked after children and care-leavers?	

Targeted responsibility (level 2) checklist

For councillors who undertake visits to children's homes (Regulation 33 visits) or who are members of a corporate parenting group, their role will be more extensive. In addition to the above, they will need to ask themselves:

Are the right structures and systems in place in order for my council to be an effective corporate parent, and are all the right partners involved?	
Am I up to date on current (and proposed) government expectations regarding the service to looked after children and care-leavers?	
Do I have access to both qualitative and quantitative information on the service, and enough knowledge to understand and evaluate this information?	
Do I know how well my council is doing in comparison with other councils and our own past performance?	
Are there sound mechanisms within my council for hearing and responding to the views of looked after children and care-leavers – and their parents/carers?	
Do I have a good picture of which needs we are meeting well and which we are failing to meet?	
Is there an action plan across the council and involving partner agencies to improve the service and to ensure it responds to changing needs?	
Do I know what our looked after children and care-leavers think about the service we are providing?	

Specialist responsibility (level 3) checklist

Finally, there will be key roles where corporate parenting is at the heart of an individual's role. The Lead Member for Children's Services and, where they have been established, the chairs of corporate parenting groups will need to work closely with the Director of Children's Services to ask themselves, in addition to all the above:

Are we providing both political and operational leadership in safeguarding and promoting the welfare of looked after children and care leavers?	
Are effective governance arrangements in place to implement any decisions regarding looked after children and care leavers across the authority and partner agencies?	
Have we undertaken an in-depth analysis of the needs of the council's care population and how far services are meeting those needs so as to inform future action?	
Is there a review process to ensure adaptation to changing needs?	
Have we made sure that the strategic plans of the children's services authority and joint plans with partner agencies meet the needs of looked after children and care-leavers?	
Are we up to date with emerging research findings and new initiatives that should inform the direction of services?	
Do we have strong links with the Children in Care Council and does that body have all the support it needs to be effective?	

Activities: Raising awareness

The activities in this section are designed to increase your knowledge, both about looked after children and your own responsibilities towards them as their corporate parent.

The activities are as follows.

1. **Test your knowledge.** A quiz to increase your understanding of the corporate parenting role.
2. **Putting corporate parenting into practice.** An exercise designed to support you in thinking about how to 'champion' the needs of looked after children in your day-to-day work
3. **What if ...? Dilemmas in corporate parenting.** A scenario-based exercise to help you consider the principles underpinning the role.

Suggested responses are provided at the end of each activity.

Looked after children: Test your knowledge

1. The majority of looked after children have been ... *Circle the correct answer.*

   (a) Removed from their parents because of abuse or neglect.

   (b) Put into care because of their socially unacceptable behaviour – that is to say, committing offences or beyond parents' control.

   (c) Placed in care because of parental illness or disability.

   (d) Placed in care because of 'absent parenting' – that is to say, there is no one to look after them.

2. The numbers of children coming into care increased by 3 per cent between 2011 and 2012. Which age group do you think accounts for the biggest increase? *Circle the correct answer.*

   Under 1   1–4 years   5–9 years   10–15 years   16 or over

3. If a looked after child is placed outside their home authority, who is responsible for paying for any mental health treatment they may need?

   ....

4. At what age does local authority responsibility for a looked after child end? *Circle the correct answer.*

   16   18   21   24   Other ....

5. Looked after children are, on average, more likely to be cautioned or convicted for an offence than other children. *Can you identify three possible reasons for this?*

   (a) ....

   (b) ....

   (c) ....

6. The School Admissions Code says that schools have to admit a looked after child if asked to do so, even if they are oversubscribed. Does this apply to the new 'free schools'?

   Yes   No

7. The longer time children spend in care, the worse their outcomes are. *Is this true or false?*

   True   False

8. What percentage of your council's care-leavers (looked after aged 16) were no longer in touch with the authority by the time they reached 19? (year ending March 2012)

   ....

9. How does this compare with the national average? *Circle the correct answer.*

   (a) More than the national average

   (b) Less than the national average

   (c) About the same

10. What percentage of your council's looked after children are taken into care through a court order, rather than by agreement with their parents?

    ....

17

Looked after children: Test your knowledge – answers

1. The majority of looked after children have been …

    (a) Removed from their parents because of abuse or neglect (62 per cent). Other reasons for children being looked after are as follows: 'family dysfunction' (14 per cent); 'family in acute stress' (9 per cent); 'absent parenting' (5 per cent); parental illness or disability (4 per cent); child's disability (3 per cent). Only 2 per cent of children are looked after because of 'socially unacceptable behaviour'. (Note: these statistics are for March 2012 and are published annually.[20])

2. The numbers of children coming into care increased by 3 per cent between 2011 and 2012. Which age group do you think accounts for the biggest increase?

    The correct answer is children under the age of one year: 5,880 children in this age group entered care in the year ending March 2012, a rise of 10 per cent. Although 10–15 year olds still constitute the largest single age group to enter care,[21] they are the only group that has declined since 2008 – all other age groups have increased. Overall, there has been a 21 per cent increase in the number of children coming into care each year since 2008.

3. If a looked after child is placed outside their home authority, who is responsible for paying for any mental health treatment they may need?

    Mental health treatment is 'secondary' care and the originating PCT (or Clinical Commissioning Group from April 2013) is responsible for providing, or paying, for it.[22]

4. At what age does local authority responsibility for a looked after child end?

    Although children may be formally discharged from care at various ages, the Children (Leaving Care) Act 2000 gave the local authority responsibility for providing ongoing practical and emotional support until the age of 21. However, if a child is still in education or training, this responsibility is extended to the age of 24 (or to the end of the agreed programme if it continues beyond 24).

5. Looked after children are, on average, more likely to be cautioned or convicted for an offence than other children. Can you identify three possible reasons for this?

    (a) Looked after children are more likely to have had adverse life experiences that increase their risk of offending behaviour.

    (b) Inadequacies in the quality of care can increase these risk factors if, for example, children live in placements where there is poor supervision by adults or they are placed with older children who are already offending. (Department for Education data[23] indicate that children in residential care are about seven times more likely to offend than those in foster care.) Other factors associated with higher rates of offending were becoming looked after due to family dysfunction/acute stress, and having experienced more than

---

20 Department for Education (2012) *Children Looked After in England: Year Ending March 2012.* Available at: http://www.education.gov.uk/researchandstatistics/statistics/a00213762/children-looked-after-las-england (accessed 14 January 2013).

21 Ibid.

22 Department of Health (2007) *Who Pays? Establishing the Responsible Commissioner.* Available at: http://www.dh.gov.uk/en/Publicationsandstatistics/Publications/PublicationsPolicyAndGuidance/DH_078466 (accessed 14 January 2013).

23 Department for Education (2011) *Outcomes for Children Looked After by Local Authorities in England: 12 Months to 30 September 2010 – Table 7.2.* Available at: http://www.education.gov.uk/researchandstatistics/datasets/a00200452/outcomes-for-children-looked-after-by-local-authorities-in-england-as-at-31-march-2011 (accessed 14 January 2013).

three placements. It also appears that children who have been looked after for only 12–18 months are at greater risk than those who have been looked after for longer, suggesting that care could be a protective factor for some.

(c) There is evidence that some looked after children are 'criminalised' within the care system, with a lower threshold for prosecution than would be the case for children living at home.

6. The School Admissions Code says that schools have to admit a looked after child if asked to do so, even if they are oversubscribed. Does this apply to the new 'free schools'?

    Yes – looked after children have priority in the school admissions arrangements. The requirements are set out in the Schools Admissions Code (DfE 2012)[24] and this applies to academies and free schools as well as schools under direct local authority control.

7. In general, the longer time children spend in care, the worse their outcomes are.

    This is false. There is a tendency to assume that care is 'bad' for children but there is research evidence to suggest that those children who are 'long looked after' (Stein 2008)[25] have more positive outcomes than those who enter the care system in adolescence. The worst outcomes are experienced by children who are 'in and out' of care, including some who are rehabilitated home after abuse.[26]

The following are sample answers. You need to find out what is happening in your own authority.

8. What percentage of your council's care-leavers (looked after aged 16) were no longer in touch with the authority by the time they reached 19? (year ending March 2012)

    13 per cent of care-leavers were reported not to be in touch with your council by the time they reached the age of 19.

9. How does this compare with the national average?

    The national average is 6 per cent so your council is twice as likely to lose contact with its care-leavers than other authorities.

10. What percentage of your council's looked after children are taken into care through a court order, rather than by agreement with their parents?

    About 74 per cent. This is unusually high. In the year ending March 2012, the average was 60 per cent and, for your region, 67 per cent.

24 Department for Education (2012) *School Admissions Code* http://www.education.gov.uk/schools/ adminandfinance/schooladmissions/a00195/current-codes-and-regulations.
25 Stein, M (2008) *Young People Leaving Care.* Highlight Series; no.240. London: National Children's Bureau.
26 Wade, J, Biehal, N, Farrelly, N and Sinclair, I (2010) *Maltreated Children in the Looked After System: A Comparison of Outcomes for Those Who Go Home and Those Who Do Not.* London: DCSF/DH.

Putting corporate parenting into practice: Exercise

Consider the following situation. What *would* you do? What *should* you do? Discuss the options and try to reach agreement about the best way forward. Make a brief note of your conclusions and the reasons for them.

You are a ward councillor and school governor of a sixth form college in an area of high deprivation. The college is drawing up its policy on the Bursary Fund scheme. Because they want the money to be targeted at those most in need, they are suggesting that the grant will be conditional on 95 per cent attendance. You are aware that the college has a cohort of looked after children living in a semi-independence scheme, but are not sure if the college knows this.

Putting corporate parenting into practice: Suggested answer

Key considerations

- Corporate parenting is different from 'ordinary' parenting in that the focus is not on forming personal relationships with individual children.
- Instead, corporate parents should remember the principle '... if this were my child ...' and champion the cause of looked after children.
- Corporate parents have a duty to question and, if necessary, to challenge aspects of the service to looked after children.
- Corporate parents must recognise the complexity of caring for looked after children, and that problems do not always have easy solutions.

What would good practice be in this situation?

The Bursary Fund scheme defines looked after children and care-leavers aged 16 to 19 (alongside other disadvantaged groups) as eligible for a bursary of £1,200 if they continue in education.

The scheme is administered by education providers and there is evidence that many eligible looked after children are not receiving it: some young people do not want their provider to know their care status or are unaware of their entitlement to claim the bursary.

There may also be particular challenges for looked after children and care-leavers in maintaining good attendance because they do not have the same support as a child in a family home would.

As the corporate parent, you should be ensuring that the systems operated by the college do not disadvantage 'your' children.

You should also make sure that the local authority is informing children of their entitlement to the bursary and supporting them to claim it.

What if ...? Dilemmas in corporate parenting: Exercise

Consider the following situations, any of which might arise for corporate parents. What *would* you do? What *should* you do? Discuss the options and try to reach agreement about the best way forward. Make a brief note of your conclusions and the reasons for them.

1. You are a ward councillor and school governor of a large comprehensive school, which is in danger of being deemed to be 'failing'. The school tell you that they are experiencing a high level of problem behaviour from a group of teenagers living in a privately run children's home local to the school. All of the children placed there are from outside your authority. One 15-year-old boy has been extremely abusive in class and generally disruptive. They want to exclude him, claiming that he is holding back the progress of other children but are worried about infringing statutory guidance about exclusion being a last resort for looked after children. The issue is to be discussed at the next governors' meeting.

2. You are a councillor and member of the corporate parenting panel. As part of your role, you undertake Regulation 33 visits to a children's home but have found it difficult to engage the children in discussion. You are also worried about the fact that staff are usually sitting in the office when you arrive rather than interacting with the children. On your last visit, you noticed a group of young men from the neighbourhood sitting on the wall smoking.

3. A sibling group of unaccompanied asylum seeking children has recently been accommodated. There is some uncertainty about the true ages of the children and their real country of origin. As a councillor, you have become aware of this through local people attending your surgery. You have asked for more detailed information about the children's accounts of their history.

4. You are a councillor who attends a 'celebration' event for looked after children. One of the children, a boy aged about nine, starts chatting to you about his experience of seeing his mother subjected to violence; about how he doesn't get on with his foster brother; how his social worker doesn't come to see him; and his wish to go home. He asks if he can talk to you again.

5. You are approached at your surgery by a black African father who complains about the fact that his teenage son has just been removed on an interim care order. He says that his son was becoming cheeky, telling lies and truanting from school. He disciplined him by hitting him with a belt, which would be accepted practice in their country of origin. His son is living in a children's home and his father perceives him as running riot. There are no African staff and the father feels that their culture is not being understood or respected. He asks you to intervene.

What if ...? Suggested responses

These suggestions are not definitive. Corporate parenting is complicated and every situation must be judged on its merits. What is in *this* child's best interests? What will be the impact of my decision on other people involved? What does the law and policy say about the action I am proposing?

1. Although you are not this child's 'corporate parent', you should still ensure that his welfare is being promoted: other children have their own parents to 'fight their corner'. This will mean checking that the school are in communication with the local authority responsible for him and that the designated teacher is aware of his care plan, including his personal education plan. He is also entitled to a fair hearing and should be properly represented. A decision to exclude him must only be taken as a last resort after other measures have been tried and failed. Although his home local authority has overall responsibility for his care, your local authority is responsible for providing him with education whilst he is placed within your area. If he is excluded, alternative measures to meet his educational needs must be put into place immediately. (Statutory guidance states that schools should be encouraged not to exclude children in care other than in the most exceptional circumstances). If there are concerns about the quality of the placement, this should be communicated to the placing authority and Ofsted.

2. Corporate parents have a duty to question, and if necessary challenge, aspects of the service to looked after children. The role should be active rather than passive: councillors acting as corporate parents are ultimately responsible for the quality of care provided. Children can be abused or poorly looked after within the care system and it is part of your role to express any doubts, even if there is no firm evidence that something is wrong. This situation needs to be raised with senior managers within children's services.

3. The children's entitlement to entry into the UK is a matter for the Immigration Authority and the Home Office. The children are entitled to a degree of privacy and there is no need for a councillor to know details of their history, although it is legitimate for you to ask general questions about compliance with council policy and cooperation with immigration enquiries.

4. Looked after children sometimes lack inhibition in talking to strangers about their circumstances: they are used to their experiences being public knowledge. It is not your role as a corporate parent to develop personal relationships with children or to come up with individual solutions. In fact, there are risks inherent in this personalised approach. Instead, you should be ensuring that services are in place to safeguard and meet the needs of the children – for example, through independent visiting schemes. You cannot meet the child's needs yourself. Children recognise this and value adults who listen to them and respond with honesty rather than those who make unrealistic promises – and fail to deliver.

5. This is a very complex issue and the challenge is to have respect for other cultures without falling into the trap of 'cultural relativism' – that is to say, applying different standards about acceptable childcare practices. A means of disciplining a child that causes 'significant harm' is grounds for a care order and the evidence would be tested in a Family Proceedings Court where all parties would be entitled to legal representation. It is not appropriate for councillors to become involved in these decisions. However, the council does have a duty to meet the cultural needs of looked after children and their families, and a councillor should be satisfied that the placements and services provided by the council meet the identified needs of looked after children both on an individual and a collective basis.

Some key points

- Corporate parenting is different from 'ordinary' parenting, in that the focus is not on forming personal relationships with individual children. In fact, there are risks inherent in this personalised approach. The emphasis should be on creating the right conditions so that individual children's needs are recognised and that services are responsive to those needs.
- Corporate parents have a duty to actively safeguard and promote the welfare of the children they look after. Where there are conflicts with the interests of constituents or others, corporate parents should remember the principle '... if this were my child ...' and champion the cause of the looked after child.
- Looked after children and their families are entitled to privacy. Growing up as a looked after child is a very public experience, with a large number of people having access to personal information. Corporate parents must respect the need to share information only where the circumstances warrant it.
- Corporate parents have a duty to question and, if necessary challenge, aspects of the service to looked after children. The role should be active rather than passive because corporate parents are ultimately responsible for the quality of the care provided.
- Corporate parents must recognise the complexity of caring for looked after children, and that problems do not always have easy solutions. Looked after children recognise this and value adults who listen to them and respond with honesty rather than those who make unrealistic promises – and fail to deliver.

A model of effective corporate parenting

Every local authority approaches the task of corporate parenting differently, but there are some key components that are essential if local arrangements are to be effective. This section:

- describes the elements of a proposed model
- suggests how to overcome challenges in implementing the model
- considers different governance arrangements
- describes the key components of a corporate parenting strategy.

Key elements of the model

This proposed model suggests a framework for the systems and processes that need to be in place if a local authority is to meet its responsibilities as a corporate parent. The model cannot be seen in isolation because consideration will need to be given to how it fits with other local authority departments, council committees and partner agencies. Corporate parenting may be delivered through different systems and structures in different authorities; however, it is suggested that the components of the model need to be in place, irrespective of the local structure, if responsibilities are to be met.

Components

Whatever structures exist in your council, **children's participation** is an essential part of the process and every local authority is expected to establish a Children in Care Council to ensure that every child has the opportunity to give their views. This may provide opportunities to involve children in drawing up the local Care Pledge. Parents, family and carers have similar contributions to make if the objective of hearing and taking into account the views of all stakeholders is to be achieved.

The group in the centre of Figure 2 carries responsibility for corporate parenting. Although it is not mandatory, most local authorities have created a specific corporate parenting board, panel or committee to fulfil this function, and different models are described in the section on governance. Its **leadership and governance** within the council must be clear – for example, there should be clarity concerning the group's powers to deploy resources and individual members must be clear about the authority they exert.

Where the group or its individual members do not possess these powers, the **decision-making processes** that will apply within their council or agency must be well defined – especially the relationship of the corporate parenting group to other management, resources, scrutiny committees and boards.

The group requires a sophisticated level of **management information** to carry out its role. This information should cover quantitative data, such as education outcomes for looked after children, and also qualitative data, such as the views of consumers of services concerning the quality and suitability of the services to meet their needs and achieve good outcomes.

The group must be able to ensure, or argue its case for the right resources in all agencies. Resources include:

- staffing
- skills
- placements and
- other support services.

Plans, strategies, policies, protocols and partnerships should assist and inform the work of the group.

Model of effective corporate parenting

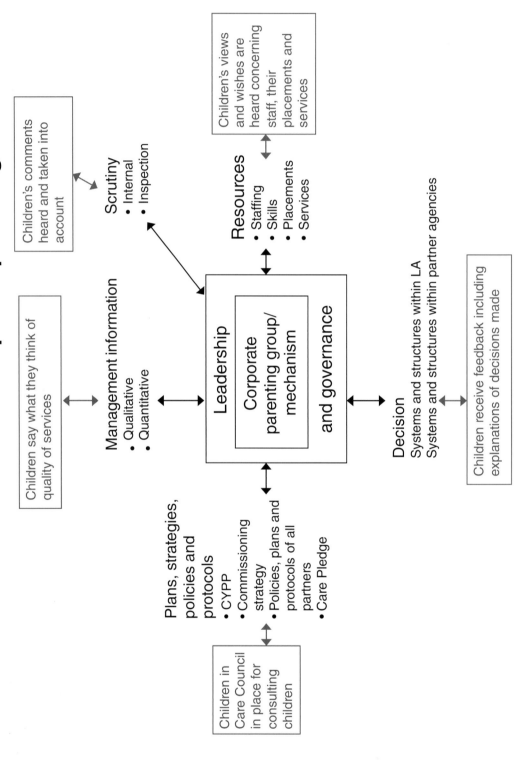

Children's comments heard and taken into account

Scrutiny
• Internal
• Inspection

Children's views and wishes are heard concerning staff, their placements and services

Resources
• Staffing
• Skills
• Placements
• Services

Children say what they think of quality of services

Management information
• Qualitative
• Quantitative

Leadership

Corporate parenting group/ mechanism

and governance

Decision

Systems and structures within LA
Systems and structures within partner agencies

Children receive feedback including explanations of decisions made

Plans, strategies, policies and protocols
• CYPP
• Commissioning strategy
• Policies, plans and protocols of all partners
• Care Pledge

Children in Care Council in place for consulting children

Implementing the model

Corporate parents have identified a number of factors that can get in the way of implementing the model of effective corporate parenting. These are presented here alongside some possible solutions.

Challenges	Possible solutions
Political differences. Changes of political leadership or tensions between political parties can 'politicise' the service for looked after children. This can interfere with the ability to develop a corporate parenting strategy, with clear priorities and action plans. It can also prevent the involvement of the Children in Care Council if the discussion is seen as unsuitable for them.	**Commit to a cross-party approach.** There is no reason why the needs of looked after children should be caught up in politics, and many councils have been able to establish a consensual approach. If members of the Children in Care Council do attend meetings, it can raise the quality of discussion by discouraging political in-fighting.
Governance and leadership are more complex with the dismantling of old structures.	**Identify where the leadership of corporate parenting will come from** within local structures. This will vary from place to place, but needs to involve all the key players – and needs to be explicit. It is good practice to develop a corporate parenting strategy that sets out the authority's vision for looked after children, and how it will be achieved.
Health reforms pose a challenge – GPs may be unaware of, or not interested in scarce needs.	**Use the JSNA** to make sure that the needs of looked after children and care-leavers are clearly articulated, and **engage the Director of Public Health** in making sure they are delivered.
Increase in numbers. Family stress/poverty and the post-baby Peter effect has led to an increase in numbers of looked after children …	**Monitor the size of case-loads** among social workers and Independent Reviewing Officers, and ensure there is a mechanism for hearing their views; and **develop a workforce strategy** to make sure that suitable staff are recruited – and retained.
… but difficulties in **prioritising** them among other pressures – and reduced resources.	**Recognise the unique status of looked after children** – they are 'your' children and the effectiveness of your service will be judged on how well they do. Good parents protect their children from economic hardship and put their needs first!
Focus on child protection and troubled families may detract from the needs of children living away from home – unless they fall within the renewed interest in adoption.	**Think holistically!** The service to looked after children cannot be considered in isolation. Good family support may prevent children coming into care – or conversely may identify children whose needs cannot be met within their family and where alternative care is needed.

Governance arrangements

A major challenge for local authorities is to get their governance arrangements for corporate parenting 'right'. Although they are not a statutory requirement, most local authorities have established a corporate parenting group to take overall responsibility.

Corporate parenting groups

In the recent round of Ofsted inspections of services for looked after children,[27] the effectiveness of these groups was sometimes commented upon. Where the group worked well it provided the leadership necessary to drive an ambitious and coherent multi-agency approach to improving outcomes for looked after children and care-leavers. Where it did not work well, services for looked after children tended to be less effective.

Ofsted identified where looked after services were considered to be good. In these authorities the corporate parenting board:

- *demonstrated a strong cross-party commitment to looked after children, by championing their rights, having high aspirations for their achievement, monitoring children's progress and challenging outcomes*

- *clearly understood its role and the responsibilities of the local authority towards looked after children, and planned for and prioritised their needs, resulting in a greater focus on improving outcomes*

- *actively engaged with their young people, for example through children in care councils that are well-established and have effective and regular links with senior management and elected members.*[28]

What is the best model for corporate parenting groups?

There is no 'right' way of establishing a corporate parenting group. Different models can be equally effective, as long as they are structured in such a way that they can fulfil the above functions. This is more difficult than it sounds: local authorities are complex organisations and the group needs to 'fit' with a range of other committees, boards and panels. Unless it is clear what the group can actually *do*, commitment is hard to maintain. The range of arrangements can include the following.

- **Corporate parenting committee.** In some councils, the corporate parenting group has the status of a formal council committee. This has the advantage of according the group a higher status than less formal groups can have. Disadvantages include the fact that council committees are open to the public, operate according to formal rules, and are therefore less likely to facilitate engagement by children and young people. This setting does not usually encourage free discussion and the outcome is often to 'note' the content of reports provided by officers rather than to drive a programme of change.
- **Children's scrutiny committee.** Part of the function of corporate parents is to monitor the service to looked after children, and this can be seen as overlapping with the council's remit

---

27   http://www.ofsted.gov.uk/children-and-families-services/for-children-and-families-services-providers/inspecting-children-and-families-services

28   Ofsted (2011) *The Annual Report of Her Majesty's Chief Inspector of Education, Children's Services and Skills 2010/11: Children's Social Care.* Available at: www.ofsted.gov.uk/resources/annualreport1011 (accessed 14 January 2013).

for scrutiny. Some councils have given responsibility for corporate parenting to their scrutiny committee or established a subgroup specifically looking at children's services. This may have the advantage that it promotes vigorous challenge but the disadvantage that scrutiny is not the same as leadership, and is unlikely to result in an effective strategy for corporate parenting.

- **Corporate parenting group/panel/board.** These are constituted specifically to take an overview of corporate parenting and have locally determined membership. Some consist only of elected members but with officers in attendance to give advice: some have mixed membership, possibly including officers from partner agencies and representatives from the Children in Care Council. The group is usually chaired by the Lead Member for Children's Services or another elected member – and opinion differs about which works best. A potential disadvantage of this model is that the status of the group may be unclear.
- **Multi-agency looked after partnership (MALAP).** Many councils have created a group of officers from the range of agencies involved in meeting the needs of looked after children and care-leavers, including health and education providers, participation workers, etc. These can share information about children's needs and coordinate services. MALAPs can work well but there needs to be clarity about how they will link with elected members. There is no reason why there should not be mixed officer and councillor membership, but some local authorities have established separate groups that link to each other.
- **Hybrid models.** These models are not mutually exclusive. Features can be combined, or in large counties there may be district groups linking to a central board.

Key ingredients

Whatever the model, the key issues to resolve are as follows.

- Who should chair the group?
- What should the membership be?
- What is the status of the group?
- What can it decide?
- Who should the group report to?
- Who should report into the group?
- How will the views of children and young people be represented?

Links with other organisations and agencies

In spite of the relaxation of government prescription, local authorities are still required to have a Director of Children's Services and a Lead Member for Children's Services. Although it is legally permissible to assign additional functions to these roles, statutory guidance requires local authorities to make sure that this will not have a detrimental effect on their ability to fulfil their responsibilities to children. Local Safeguarding Children Boards also remain unchanged.

New requirements for local authorities are the creation of the post of Director of Public Health, previously an NHS role, and the establishment of a Health and Well-being Board. The previous requirement to have a Children's Trust Board has been withdrawn. Within this broad context, local authorities can determine their own governance arrangements for services to children.

In determining what governance arrangements will work best, the groups/committees illustrated in Figure 3 will need to be considered.

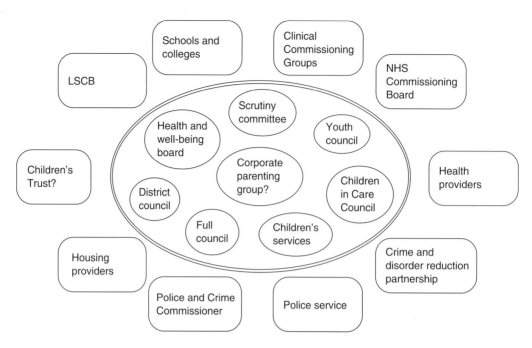

Figure 2: A coherent approach to governance: who needs to be included?

Task

Consider your local arrangements in relation to these bodies and consider the following.

◼ Does the council have a structure for the governance of corporate parenting that includes all the bodies in the figure?

◼ Are the lines of accountability clear?

What happens elsewhere?

Individual authorities may also create their own local boards. For example, **North Somerset** has established a People and Communities Board. This brings together the previous Children and Families Partnership, the Health and Well-being Partnership and the Safer, Stronger Partnership, and has a number of statutory duties across all these work areas. **Wiltshire** has established 18 area boards to make decisions about local services. In **Bristol**, they have established a Children's Outcomes Board as a sub-group of the Health and Well-being Board.

The need to determine governance structures does not apply only to adult bodies: the links between the Children in Care Council and other bodies representing children and young people will need to be determined. Although looked after children deserve special consideration, many of their interests will overlap with those of other local children. For example, they will all have views on the accessibility of transport and leisure activities.

In **Bristol**, the Youth Select Committee is linked to the Children in Care Council for this reason and in **Torbay**, there is an overall participation strategy with the voice of looked after children as one strand.

Finally, the links between children's and adults' groups will need to be established, particularly the Children in Care Council and corporate parenting group. Many authorities are looking at the best way of doing this.

In **Wiltshire** the meeting of the corporate parenting group is divided into two sections: one where the more formal items are discussed and an informal session in which children participate.

In **Wokingham**, the Corporate Parenting Board has created a 'link role' for councillors.

Elected members take on a specific linking role on behalf of the Corporate Parenting Board in one or more of the following areas:

- housing/care-leavers
- education
- health
- placements and short breaks
- leisure/social
- listening to children/young people.

A local authority officer from within Children's Services has been identified as the point of contact for each elected member. The elected member and the officer meet regularly to discuss their particular area.

Key components of a corporate parenting strategy

There is no statutory requirement to have a specific strategy for corporate parenting, but where a strategy has been developed it demonstrates that the local authority is not only committed to looked after children but has a vision about what it wants to achieve. It provides a focal point for all agencies, staff, and children and young people to understand what the objectives for the service are – and to hold the council to account if they are not delivered.

There is no template for a corporate parenting strategy. It is important for it to be owned locally, so the process of drafting, agreeing and reviewing the strategy should be an inclusive one. Any 'good' strategy will include as a minimum a statement of objectives and how these will be achieved and reviewed, but some councils have taken the opportunity to set out a broader vision and to give a voice to children and young people affected by the strategy.

Solihull's corporate parenting strategy for 2011–15 starts with a letter from a care-leaver to Solihull's corporate parents telling them what children in care need from them.[29] Children's voices are apparent throughout the document and the strategy is clearly linked to the Care Pledge, or promise, that the council has made. Each aspect of the promise details how it will be implemented and how progress will be measured.

Tameside's strategy is similarly specific, with eight clear objectives for improving the service before, during and after children's journey through care.[30] It also sets out the principles underpinning the objectives so that the committed stance of corporate parents is explicit. The actions that are described are detailed and concrete, such as working with the local sports trust to access their facilities and providing children over 14 with a laptop.

Wokingham's strategy was presented to the full council and explains what being a corporate parent means, drawing on research findings and the legal framework.[31] It also refers to inspection findings and the way these influenced decisions about the areas for improvement. A number of the priorities relate to more effective governance and involvement by children and young people rather than direct services, and a minimum set of expectations for all corporate parents is included.

---

29 Solihull Metropolitan Borough Council (2011) *Corporate Parenting Strategy, 2011 to 2015*. Available at: http://www.solihull.gov.uk/akssolihull/images/att33506.pdf (accessed 15 January 2013).

30 Tameside Metropolitan Borough Council (2012) *Corporate Parenting Strategy for Looked after Children 2012–2015*. Available at: www.tameside.gov.uk/lac/strategy/1215.pdf (accessed 15 January 2013).

31 Wokingham Borough Council (2012) *Corporate Parenting Board Strategy*. Available at: http://bit.ly/V3Cspl (accessed 22 January 2013).

Suggested headings

The following list is not definitive, but could be used as a starting point in drafting a corporate parenting strategy.

1. Introductory statement about the council's vision and commitment to corporate parenting.
2. Messages/letter for corporate parents from looked after children.
3. Explanation of corporate parenting and how it works in this council.
   - Who has lead responsibility within the local authority and partner agencies?
   - Roles and responsibilities of everyone involved and the different levels of responsibility.
   - The structural arrangements for developing and monitoring the corporate parenting strategy, including the terms of reference of relevant groups and how they link together.
4. Entitlements of looked after children and the local authority Care Pledge.
5. Analysis of the local population of children on the edge of care, looked after children and care-leavers, including:
   - statistical profile about who they are and where they are placed
   - an analysis of their needs
   - information about outcomes
   - children's views and wishes
   - description of current services and initiatives within the council and partner agencies, including arrangements for commissioning and review
   - current concerns, such as children missing from care or recurrent themes within complaints.
6. Identification, arising from the above, of:
   - what the council and partners are doing well
   - what improvements need to be made
   - specific objectives and priorities for the next three years.
7. Action Plan describing how the objectives will be achieved, including timescales, who is responsible and the desired outcomes.

Working with children and young people

> *If I was in charge of social services, I'd listen to them [people in care] first, see what they've got to say. I can't just make the rules on what I think is best for them.*
>
> (Young person)[32]

An essential part of being an effective corporate parent is good communication with the children and young people you are looking after. There are many different ways of doing this but it is something that children are entitled to. They should be able to express their views, and to have them taken seriously, both with regard to their own lives and the service for looked after children in general.

This section contains:

■ an introduction to working with children and young people, including ways of ensuring that this happens, and the role of the Care Pledge
■ a summary of what children have said about the experience of having a corporate parent
■ 10 top tips for corporate parents from A National Voice, expressing the views of children in care.

Partnership with your Children in Care Council

Looked after children have a statutory entitlement to have their views taken into account and many councils have employed participation workers or children's rights workers to support children and young people in gaining a voice. The Children's Rights Director has produced a guide for young people to support them in knowing what they can expect from their corporate parents.[33]

Corporate parents are not expected to get involved with individual children's cases – and there are risks associated with doing so – but they should be aware that the principle of participation should extend throughout all aspects of children's experiences in the care system. Not all children will choose to be members of the Children in Care Council but they should *all* have a voice in their own care plan and the way this is implemented on a day-to-day basis. The council's Independent Reviewing Officers have a statutory responsibility to make sure this happens and corporate parents should satisfy themselves that they are supported in this role.

Lancashire have developed *Golden Rules for Corporate Parenting Board Reports and Presentations*, with a view to making sure that these are accessible for all. In the words of young people, all presentations should be 'interesting', 'colourful', 'understandable' and 'loud, clear and inspirational'![36]

---

32 Voice For the Child in Care (2004) *Start With the Child, Stay With the Child: A Blueprint for a Child-centred Approach to Children and Young People in Public Care.* London: Voice.

33 Children's Rights Director (2012) *Young People's Guide to Good Corporate Parents.* Available at: https://www.rights4me.org/en/home/library/guides/guide-young-persons-guide-to-good-corporate-parents.aspx (accessed 15 January 2013).

34 http://www3.lancashire.gov.uk/corporate/web/view.asp?siteid=4183&pageid=17628&e=e

Looked after children and care-leavers should also be given the opportunity to comment on the service more generally, and councils are expected to facilitate this. Most councils have established Children in Care Councils to fulfil this expectation, but work undertaken by A National Voice (ANV) suggests that their effectiveness is variable.[35] Overall, Children in Care Councils were most effective when they had:

- close links with the Director of Children's Services and elected members
- developed terms of reference or a constitution.

Most Children in Care Councils were unclear about whether they had a budget and, if so, where it came from and what it could be spent on. ANV has summarised key messages in the *Ten Top Tips for Corporate Parents* included in these resources.

Creating the right framework

Although it is not the only factor in establishing a good working relationship, it is important to determine the structures that will enable communication between corporate parents and the children they look after. There is no universal way of doing this that will work for every council, but whatever model is chosen it should be transparent and reflected in the terms of reference of all relevant groups.

Different councils have gone about this in different ways, and approaches are not mutually exclusive or static. Some councils have started with formalised and limited involvement between corporate parents and looked after children, but evolved this further once mutual trust and respect had been established. People may be worried that corporate parenting board meetings will be 'boring' for children and young people, although the experience of authorities that have opened their meetings have found that this is not necessarily the case. **Ealing Council** has embraced this model for a number of years, and feels that is has worked well.

> **Barnet**'s corporate parenting group has a designated slot at the beginning of meetings for representatives of the Children in Care Council, but also invites them to stay for the rest of the agenda if they want to.

Possible approaches include the following.

1. Membership of the corporate parenting panel is open to representatives of the Children in Care Council.
2. Formalised links are developed between the corporate parenting group and the Children in Care Council. This can take the form of a programme of joint meetings; a mechanism for feeding agenda items into each other's meetings; attendance by children's participation workers at the corporate parenting group; exchange of meeting minutes; synchronicity of meetings.
3. Joint activities between corporate parents and the Children in Care Council. Many councils have developed their Care Pledge to looked after children in partnership with their Children in Care Council, but there is scope for other project work that could strengthen the relationship. For example, the Children in Care Council could be involved in a thematic scrutiny of aspects of the service, and could undertake joint Regulation 33 visits with corporate parents or help to develop information about services.

---

35 A National Voice (2011) *CiCC Mapping Project 2010–11*. Available at: http://www.anationalvoice.org/work/reports/cicc-mapping-project-2010-11 (accessed 15 January 2013).

It is not all about meetings: there are many ways of involving children and young people. Some authorities are successfully using social media such as Facebook and Twitter, and **Staffordshire** and **Wiltshire** are happy to share how they went about this. **West Sussex** commissioned a theatre group to work with their looked after children and were positive about the outcome.

In **Northamptonshire**, children and young people in care and care-leavers have continued to be involved in the design, delivery and evaluation of services, including:

- a consultation event on health and health assessments
- the redesign of the pathway plan for 16+
- development of a Care-Leavers Forum
- care-leavers drop-in service (one-stop shop)
- design of leaving care website
- voluntary work, work experience and apprenticeship schemes
- membership of the Making a Positive Contribution subgroup includes care-leavers
- designing the 'Coming into care' pack
- daily living project.

It is also important to remember that children in the looked after system have the same interests and preoccupations as other children. There should be mechanisms for engaging them in other local consultative groups, such as school councils, youth parliaments and health watch groups.

The Care Pledge

There is an expectation that councils will develop a pledge for their looked after children and care-leavers, setting out their commitments.[36] There is no template for what the Care Pledge should contain, or any mandatory process for how it should be developed or reviewed. Most councils have developed a leaflet, in partnership with the Children in Care Council, and have disseminated it to their looked after children and care-leavers, but many acknowledge that it is not a dynamic document that informs their day-to-day work.

Some Care Pledges are really only a list of what the council must provide anyway, such as entitlement to an allocated social worker and a care plan. This may be a useful summary but is not a substitute for a local set of commitments, particularly as the government has responded to requests from children and young people by issuing documents setting out the entitlements of looked after children and care-leavers.[37] These are the things to which looked after children and care-leavers are entitled to by right, whichever council is responsible for their care.

A challenge for individual councils is to make their own Pledge meaningful – a live document setting out specific commitments that can be used by young people to hold their corporate parent to account. The following questions can be used to reflect on your own council's Care Pledge and to identify any work needed to revitalise it.

- Is your Pledge just a repetition of children's statutory entitlements or does it also include some commitments that are local to your service?
- If it does include statutory entitlements, does it make it clear that this is what they are?

---

36 Department for Education and Skills (2007) *Care Matters: Time for Change.* Norwich: The Stationery Office.
37 Department for Education (2012) *Entitlements for Children in Care and Care Leavers.* Available at: http://www.education.gov.uk/childrenandyoungpeople/families/childrenincare/a00208882/leavers (accessed 15 January 2013).

- Are the promises made in the Pledge specific and measurable rather than vague and aspirational? For example, 'We will provide you with a free leisure pass' rather than 'We will help you to pursue your outside interests'.
- Is there a regular process for checking with children and young people whether they consider that the Pledge has been delivered?
- Is there a timescale and process for refreshing and updating the Pledge?
- Have you checked that all corporate parents, looked after children and care-leavers are aware of the Pledge?

In **Calderdale**, a 'Dear Corporate Parent' letter has been developed and promoted by Independent Reviewing Officers at looked after children reviews in order to offer children a direct feedback route to the corporate parenting panel.

Finally, please do not refer to looked after children as 'LAC'! It denies their status as individuals with unique personalities and needs.

Children's experience of having a corporate parent

The Children's Rights Director recently consulted looked after children about their experience of having a corporate parent.[38] Their views reinforced the findings from other studies: that looked after children want to be seen as individuals and valued in their own right rather than being looked after in an impersonal way. They want to be cared about, not just cared for, but corporate parents are not always successful at this.

Having care plans, meetings and case files

Children identified a number of ways in which being cared for by a corporate parent made them 'different'. One very obvious difference was the structured approach to their care. Looked after children were very aware that having a 'care plan', review meetings and formal medicals were not things that happened within normal family life. Although they could understand the reasons for this difference, it made life difficult and uncomfortable at times. They had to deal with a large number of adults having a say in their life.

Financial factors

The amount of money directly available to looked after children, or for their carers to spend on them, were seen as marking them out as different. Some thought they had more money, others less, and they perceived there to be discrepancies between local authorities or placements in their approach to finances. Worryingly, cost was seen as the biggest factor in decisions made by their local authority about what should happen to them and where they should be placed.

Bureaucratic processes for 'permission'

Looked after children found it frustrating to have to get permission from their corporate parent to do everyday things, such as go on a school trip or stay with friends. Residential or foster carers did not usually seem to have delegated authority to authorise these things and it could be a long process to get local authority permission. To quote one looked after child,

> *'You can't just go over to your friend's house ... it takes three to six months for police checks. Other people just go.'*[39]

This problem has been recognised by the government and they have written to local authorities about delegating authority to carers – provided there are no individual circumstances that would be against the interests of a particular child.

---

38   Children's Rights Director (2011) *Having Corporate Parents: 'We're Not Treated Like Children, We're a Case'.* Available at: https://www.rights4me.org/home/library/reports/report-having-corporate-parents.aspx (accessed 15 January 2013).
39   Ibid.

Being treated differently at school

Children described being treated differently not only by education staff but also by other children. At times this could be out of curiosity – being seen as 'weird' – or it could be that people were 'too nice'. Getting extra resources or attention made looked after children stand out and they were not always comfortable with this. It could be particularly difficult if expectations about the transition to independent living did not correspond to their educational status. Trying to pursue education while living alone, without the support of residential or foster carers, is a big challenge.

Leaving care early to live on your own

In spite of the additional support and protectiveness described above, looked after children are still expected to make the transition to independent living sooner than their peers. In the words of one looked after child:

> *'You're made to move out to get a flat at 16, and at that age you think "great", but you're not ready.'*[40]

This was a source of anxiety for some children, although others were positive about the fact that they were entitled to receive help with accommodation when they left care.

Moving from place to place

The importance of placement stability is well recognised, and looked after children confirm how stressful it can be to move from place to place:

> *'There is no good thing about moving. It affected me. I couldn't think straight. We're like objects.'*[41]

For some, moves had been positive and they recognised that staying in an inadequate placement was not the solution. The way that moves take place could be better, and children described receiving little warning of a move, or they stressed the need for more information – or choice – about where they were going.

Multiple professionals and disrupted relationships

Children describe a range of different professionals involved in their lives, including not only social workers and carers but also Independent Reviewing Officers, advocates and independent visitors. Their views on these differed according to their own experiences but most thought they could be a useful source of support – as long as there were not too many of them.

---

40   Ibid.
41   Ibid.

Having a Children in Care Council and a Care Pledge

Although not all looked after children are aware of these, they are generally seen as positive and empowering. As one looked after child explained:

> 'We have participation meetings and we can ask, "Why aren't we getting this?" When you point out things that are wrong, you can get things changed. It's good.'[42]

Three-quarters of children who commented thought that the Children in Care Council had made a difference – more so than the local Care Pledge.

---

42   Ibid.

a national voice

Ten Top Tips for Corporate Parents
What Young People From CiCCs Say...

1. Get involved with important events for young people such as awards ceremonies and events which celebrate and recognise achievement.
2. Only attend CiCC meetings when invited. This is their council; they should decide who is required at meetings.
3. If agreed with young people, attend their outings, events and residentials, and dress down...don't always be the formal one.
4. Keep your young people informed of decisions being made as a result of their requests. If the decisions don't go in their favour, make sure you fully explain why; don't just give them a refusal.
5. If you can't attend a meeting to give feedback in person, consider using other methods – do you have time for a Skype call (it's free, and really easy to set up!) or a phone meeting? Could you send a DVD with a pre-recorded message?
6. Consider holding a session with your CiCC dedicated to getting to know each other: they can ask you questions about yourself and your role, and you can find out more about them. Try ice-breaker exercises – they do work!
7. Arrange for young people from your CiCC to deliver some tips or training to the Corporate Parenting Board on how to relate to young people. Even better, let some CiCC members shadow you for a day and vice versa; this will help you to relate to each other.
8. Plan, review and monitor your Pledge routinely, and make sure you're sticking to the promises you've made.
9. Have at least one member of your CiCC sit on the Corporate Parenting Board as a regular member. They may need support to do this.
10. When making any decisions, **always** ask yourself 'Would this be good enough for my child?'

Head Office: Central Hall - Oldham Street - Manchester - M1 1JQ
t: 0161-237-5577   e: info@anationalvoice.org
www.anationalvoice.org Charity No: 1120149 Company Limited by Guarantee No: 5760207
Registered in England

Is the service good enough?

A key role for elected members in their capacity as corporate parents is to determine whether the service to looked after children provided by their council is good enough. As a benchmark , you should be asking yourselves whether you would consider it good enough for your own child. Elected members are ultimately accountable for the quality of the service. The challenge is: how will you *know*?

This section contains:

- consideration of how corporate parents can make sure they have the 'right' information
- two exercises to support corporate parents in making judgements on the basis of
    - statistical information
    - qualitative information
- suggestions about the process for determining priorities for action.

Evaluating the service delivered by the council to looked after children is not just the responsibility of scrutiny committees. 'Real' parents don't leave it to others to decide whether their child is doing well: they keep a close eye on their welfare and ask searching questions to decide if they need to act. Similarly, the role of corporate parent is not a passive one. They should be actively challenging and driving change where outcomes could be improved.

Lead Members and corporate parenting groups will probably receive reports from officers containing data about the numbers and profile of children looked after by the council, and some of their outcomes. This can be difficult to make sense of. Is a 62 per cent success rate in GCSEs good or bad? The answer will usually be – it depends. Corporate parents will need to know the answers to the following questions.

- Was this higher or lower than last year? What are the trends?
- How does it compare with the England average for looked after children or with other comparable councils?
- How does it compare with the performance of other local children who are not looked after?
- Is there any data that shows the children's rate of improvement since they came into care?
- How does children's actual attainment compare with their projected outcomes – and with their potential?

In addition to these statistical questions, however, there will need to be a dialogue if data is to make sense. There may be a cohort of particularly academic children going through the system that are driving up outcome performance but masking the fact that other children are achieving poorly. Elected members are dependent on officers for this back-story. It is important that a climate of trust be established and that elected members make it clear that they want the bad news as well as the good.

However good statistical reports are, there is also a need to hear other types of information. A 'good' performance in terms of placement stability is only positive if the children are thriving in those placements. Outcomes such as a sense of being valued and having hope for the future cannot be statistically measured, and elected members will need another way of finding out. For every aspect of the service that corporate parents want to consider, there will be more than one source of information. The 'experts' will always be the children, carers and front-line staff who are experiencing the service at first hand and there must be effective methods in place to hear from them directly. Apart from face-to-face contact, valuable sources of information could be an analysis of any complaints that have been made about the service, exit interviews with children leaving care, staff surveys and the annual report from the Independent Reviewing Officer.

This section includes a number of materials that can be used to help you to reflect on whether the service is good enough – and, if so, whether it could be even better.

Getting the 'right' statistical information

Corporate parents need to know how well their children are doing before they can decide if action is needed to improve their outcomes. Most corporate parenting groups receive regular statistical reports from officers, but these vary in usefulness. Some groups are drowning in data, such as monthly updates on the numbers of children who have entered or left the care system (which tells them very little), while others receive timely and valuable information that can be used to set new objectives and review the effectiveness of services.

For example, the Virtual School head may report on the children's exam results every September, accompanied by data on last year's results and those of comparator authorities. Where there are reasons for changes in performance, such as a particular cohort known to have specific difficulties, this explanation should be provided. This does not mean that corporate parents have to accept the explanation at face value – they may want to ask for supporting information. A healthy scepticism and a willingness to ask what the data *means* are useful attributes for corporate parenting groups. Good information does not leave the reader thinking: 'So what?'

A useful starting point is for councillors to agree with officers which data they want to see and when. A thematic approach to reporting is more manageable than looking at all the data at every meeting. Every council routinely collects data and submits it to the Department for Education. This includes two main types of data:

- *demographic* data on the profile of all the council's looked after children
- *outcome* data on children who have been looked after for 12 months or more.

The data is published annually,[43] allowing national, regional and local comparisons. Data on past performance is also provided so that trends can be analysed. Local authorities are matched to others with similar demographics because it can be misleading to compare areas of deprivation with those of affluence, and every local authority should know who its comparators are.

The timescale for publishing the data means that it is several months old when it becomes publically available, but corporate parenting groups can request it from their officers at any point and in whatever format they find useful. They can also ask for additional levels of analysis to be undertaken. For example, they may want to know how attainment compares across children placed in local as opposed to out-of-authority placements.

The Department for Education has undertaken this more detailed analysis of certain aspects of national performance. So far these are attainment,[44] care-leavers,[45] children's homes,[46] and adoption and special guardianship.[47] These are a useful resource for councils wanting to consider their performance in more depth.

---

43 http://www.education.gov.uk/researchandstatistics/statistics/statistics-by-topic/childrenandfamilies/ lookedafterchildren (accessed 16 January 2013).

44 http://www.education.gov.uk/childrenandyoungpeople/families/childrenincare/a00192332/raising-the-aspirations-and-educational-outcomes-of-looked-after-children-a-data-tool-for-local-authorities (accessed 16 January 2013).

45 http://www.education.gov.uk/childrenandyoungpeople/families/childrenincare/a00216209/care-leavers-data-pack (accessed 16 January 2013).

46 http://www.education.gov.uk/childrenandyoungpeople/families/childrenincare/childrenshomes/a00192000/ childrens-homes-data-pack (accessed 16 January 2013).

47 http://www.education.gov.uk/childrenandyoungpeople/families/adoption/b0076713/datapack (accessed 16 January 2013).

Starting in 2012, government has produced Adoption Scorecards.[48] These show, against three key indicators, how swiftly children are placed for adoption in each local authority area. In future, they will also show the speed of the response to prospective adopters.

What data is routinely collected?

Although data collection requirements change over time as central government identifies new priorities, such as the current focus on adoption, the following is a summary of the information that is currently collected.

Profile

- Children looked after at 31 March (the data year runs from 1 April 1 to 31 March) by gender, age, category of need, ethnic origin, legal status and placement.
- Children who started – and ceased – to be looked after during the year, broken down into the above categories.
- Unaccompanied asylum-seeking children looked after by gender, age, category of need and ethnic origin.
- Mothers aged 12 years old and over looked after by age, category of need, ethnic origin, placement and region.
- Children looked after during the year under at least one agreed series of short-term placements by gender, age, placement and category of need.

Placement

- Children looked after by placement, distance between home and placement, locality of placement, placement provider and whether placement is in or out of a local authority's area.
- Placement stability and number of placements.

Adoption

- Looked after children who were adopted during the year by gender, age, ethnic origin, duration of the adoption process, etc.
- Children for whom the local authority has made the decision that the child should be placed for adoption, those placed and waiting for adoption and details of children where the decision to be placed for adoption has been reversed.

Care-leavers

- Children now aged 19 years old who were looked after when aged 16 years by gender, accommodation and activity, including whether they are still in touch with the authority.

---

48 http://www.education.gov.uk/childrenandyoungpeople/families/adoption/a00208817/adoption-scorecards (accessed 16 January 2013).

Reviews

- Children looked after who were required to have a review during the year, by method of participation at the last review.

Attainment

- Key Stage 1 eligibility and performance of children who have been looked after continuously for at least 12 months, by gender.
- Key Stage 2 eligibility and performance of children who have been looked after continuously for at least 12 months, by gender.
- Key Stage 4 eligibility and performance of children who have been looked after continuously for at least 12 months, by gender.
- School sessions missed due to absences.
- Proportion of school age looked after children who were attending a school that was assessed as being below the floor targets at Key Stage 2 or Key Stage 4.

Other outcomes

- Offending by children who had been looked after continuously for at least 12 months, by age and gender.
- Substance misuse by children who had been looked after continuously for at least 12 months, by age and gender.
- Education and employment status of children who had been looked after continuously for at least 12 months, following completion of National Curriculum Year 11.
- Children missing from care.

Health

- Healthcare of children who had been looked after continuously for at least 12 months: immunisations, dental checks and health assessments.
- Development assessments of children aged 5 or under who had been looked after continuously for at least 12 months.
- Average score for children looked after for whom a Strengths and Difficulties Questionnaire (SDQ) was completed.

Corporate parenting groups will need to agree with officers how this information will be presented to them and in what format. Good information does not leave the reader thinking: 'So what?'.

> Some councils have developed a local 'scorecard' with the data broken down into categories that enable elected members to evaluate the information, and to set local targets for improvement. An example of **Kent**'s scorecard is provided as an example on the NCB website for corporate parents.

Exercise: Making sense of performance data

Aims

This exercise is designed to develop the skill of corporate parents in making sense of statistical data by working through practical examples. Sample data that is routinely collected by councils is presented so that you can consider possible reasons for aspects of the performance and plan how enquiries could be taken forward.

Key points

There are no right or wrong answers. The pattern of performance illustrated by the data could be an indication of good or bad practice – or neither. There could be demographic factors that make this council different from others. The important point is to understand the range of possible explanations, to know how to seek additional information to test out those explanations, and to act to address any weaknesses that are then revealed.

Possible reasons – and actions to find out more – are offered following each example.

Example 1: Age profile in Thistledon

The following information is contained within a report to the corporate parenting forum.

Age profile of Thistledon's looked after children (%)

Under 1	1–4	5–9	10–15	16 and over	
5	26	25	33	10	Thistledon
6	18	18	37	21	England
5	21	21	36	16	Region

This data would suggest that Thistledon has a lower percentage of children aged 16 and over than other authorities.

1. **What might the reasons for this be?** Discuss and list all the possible explanations you can think of.

2. **What do you want your officers to do?** Set out the specific actions to be taken, including who is responsible, what the timescale is and how you will review the work.

Age profile in Thistledon: Possible reasons and actions to find out more

Possible reasons

Note that the answer may be a combination of all/some of these:

a)   Discharging higher than average numbers of 16/17 year olds from care.
b)   Not admitting vulnerable homeless 16/17 year olds to care.
c)   Lower numbers entering care in this cohort at a younger age leading to lower numbers now.
d)   Unusual demographics of Thistledon.
e)   Influx of children in another age group making this percentage seem low in comparison with other local authorities and nationally.
f)   This year is just different from all other years – an anomaly.
g)   Targeted preventive services are helping families remain together at points of crisis in adolescence.

What do you want your officers to do?

a)   Ask officers about:
   ■   policy and practice regarding discharge from care prior to 18
   ■   details of age of discharge from care for 16–18 year olds and comparisons with national/ regional data.
b)   Ask officers to check policy and practice concerning the 'Southwark judgement' to ensure the law about accommodating vulnerable 16/17 year olds is being adhered to.
c)   Ask officers if there is data available to prove/disprove the hypothesis that low numbers of older children are coming into the system.
d)   Ask officers for details of demographics and whether there is anything unusual about this cohort.
e)   Compare your data with other local authorities with similar numbers and demographics.
f)   Compare your own data for previous years to establish if this is a trend.

Apart from your officers, your carers and young people in care are likely to have views about possible reasons. You could consult the Children in Care Council about what they think, based on their own experience and from talking with other looked after young people and care-leavers.

Example 2: Contact with care-leavers in Dunshire

Percentage of 19 year olds who were in care at the age of 16 and who are still in touch with the local authority

% still in touch	
74	Dunshire
94	England
80	Region

This data would suggest that Dunshire is less likely to maintain contact with care-leavers than other authorities.

1. **What might the reasons for this be?** Discuss and list all the possible explanations you can think of.

2. **What do you want your officers to do?** Set out the specific actions to be taken, including who is responsible, what the timescale is and how you will review the work.

Contact with care-leavers in Dunshire: Possible reasons and actions to find out more

Possible reasons

Note that the answer may be a combination of all/some of these:

a) Discharging children from care at 16/17 years so there is more opportunity for them to drift away.
b) Poor quality or under-resourced leaving care services.
c) A large number of out-of-authority placements so that care-leavers have lost local relationships.
d) Problems with collecting or analysing accurate data.
e) This year is just different from all other years – an anomaly or an unusual cohort.
f) Care-leavers are receiving good support from other services and do not rely on the local authority.
g) A cohort of unaccompanied asylum seekers who disappear aged 18 to avoid the threat of being returned to their country of origin.

What do you want your officers to do?

a) Ask officers about:
   - policy and practice regarding discharge from care prior to 18
   - services provided for care-leavers in comparison with other local authorities.
b) Ask officers if there is data available to prove/disprove these hypotheses.
c) Ask officers for details of demographics and whether there is anything unusual about this cohort.
d) Compare your data with other local authorities with similar numbers and demographics.
e) Compare your own data for previous years to establish if this is a trend.

Apart from your officers, your carers and young people in care are likely to have views about possible reasons. You could consult the Children in Care Council about what they think, based on their own experience and from talking with other looked after young people and care-leavers.

Example 3: Health performance in Hightown

Percentage of children who have been looked after for
12 months or more with up-to-date healthcare

% with up-to-date immunisations	% with up-to-date dental checks	% with up-to-date health assessments	
93	59	66	Hightown
79	82	84	England

The data suggest that health services in Hightown are more successful than the national average in getting children immunised but markedly less successful at ensuring they have dental and health checks.

1. **What might the reasons for this be?** Discuss and list all the possible explanations you can think of.

2. **What do you want your officers to do?** Set out the specific actions to be taken, including who is responsible, what the timescale is and how you will review the work.

Health performance in Hightown: Possible reasons and actions to find out more

Possible reasons

Note that the answer may be a combination of all/some of these:

a) A large number of out-of-authority placements mean that the council is having to negotiate for health assessments to be done by other NHS trusts, and they are failing to prioritise these.
b) There are insufficient designated doctors and nurses to ensure that looked after children are getting the service they need.
c) There may be a shortage of local dentists offering NHS treatment, or they may not want to take on temporary patients.
d) Local foster carers and residential workers have good links with primary health services so are easily able to get children immunised.
e) Children have had bad experiences with local health or dental practitioners so are reluctant to attend.
f) The Director of Public Health has not recognised the needs of looked after children or afforded them any priority.

What do you want your officers to do?

a) Ask officers about the arrangements for undertaking health assessments, including children placed out of the authority.
b) Put the problem to the Director of Public Health and engage her/him in discussion about how to improve performance.
c) Make sure the JSNA includes data on looked after children's health.
d) Ask the designated doctor and nurse to examine the reasons for the poor performance and prepare a report for the corporate parenting group.
e) Ask what other authorities are doing to persuade children to attend health assessments and to make them more accessible.
f) Compare your data with other local authorities with similar numbers and demographics.
g) Compare your own data for previous years to establish if this is a trend.

Apart from your officers, your carers and young people in care are likely to have views about possible reasons. You could consult the Children in Care Council about what they think, based on their own experience and from talking with other looked after young people and care-leavers.

Exercise: Evaluating quality – how do you *know* if it's good enough?

Although it is important to focus on overall outcomes based on the performance data that officers provide, there will also be instances where doubts are raised about children's experiences in care. Elected members often ask about how they can really know what is going on – and whether they can trust what senior officers tell them.

The key points that these scenarios illustrate are:

- that the role of councillors is to satisfy themselves that complaints have been investigated properly, not to get directly involved in the investigation
- that it is important to check out information from a number of different sources, such as relevant inspection reports, the IRO report, Children in Care Council consultations and analysis of complaints.

Scenario 1: Rochester Place Children's Home

Concern

This six-bedded children's home is run by your authority and takes children aged 12–16 for assessment and short-term care.

Mia, aged 13, is placed in Rochester Place because her single father felt unable to control her. She sometimes stayed out all night, was drinking with older teenagers and was thought to be at risk of sexual exploitation. The staff at the children's home are also having difficulty in coping with this behaviour.

Mia's father has made a formal complaint because he noticed a graze-like mark on her cheek. Mia said it was caused when staff restrained her to stop her going out. He queried this with staff, who confirmed they had restrained her and the mark was a 'carpet burn' as a result of her resisting when being held on the floor. They said they had restrained her to prevent her coming to harm because she wanted to go out at 11pm to meet a man in his 20s.

Supporting information

- **Ofsted** has rated the home 'satisfactory'.
- **Regulation 33 visits**. The home is visited regularly by elected members on a rota basis. They have reported some difficulties in getting the children to engage with them and say the home can feel chaotic, with staff spending most of their time in the office.
- **Annual IRO report**. The IRO manager has expressed a view that the council does not have sufficient high quality placements, particularly for teenagers. The council has been pursuing a policy of reducing the use of out-of-authority placements.

Action

The complaint raised by Mia's father is being formally investigated but he has also asked his ward councillor to get involved. The councillor has raised the matter with the Lead Member for Children's Services. He, in turn, has asked the Director of Children's Services (DCS) for advice, and has been told that Rochester Place provides a reasonable standard of care, overall, for a challenging group of children.

Task

Consider how the Lead Member could arrive at a judgement about:

1. Whether the standard of care is good enough for *this* child.
2. Whether the case raises wider issues about policy and practice in the authority.
3. What action might need to be taken.

Scenario 1: Rochester Place Children's Home key points

This is a complicated situation, and there may well be contradictory conclusions even after a thorough investigation.

- The role of councillors is to satisfy themselves that complaints have been investigated properly, not to get directly involved in the investigation. That is a task for officers.
- The Director of Children's Services could be correct in asserting that the home is operating to an acceptable standard – but could also be wrong. There is enough information here to raise concerns.
- In relation to this child:
  - Is Mia in the most suitable placement? This home may not be able to meet her current needs and she could be better placed somewhere with more structure or therapeutic input.
  - Has there been a thorough assessment of Mia's vulnerability to sexual exploitation?
  - Do staff need to do something different in the way they work with Mia? For example, has she got a behaviour management plan that has been developed in partnership between Mia and staff?
- In relation to broader issues of policy and practice:
  - Is the council satisfied with its processes for undertaking Regulation 33 visits? Have councillors got the necessary knowledge and skills to fulfil the role effectively? For example, are they a consistent group so that children can develop a relationship of trust with them; do they know what they are looking for?
  - What is the council's policy on physical restraint? Do staff use an accredited method and have they all been trained in its use? Is practice monitored within each home and across the council as a whole?
  - What did Ofsted consider to be the home's shortcomings and are these being addressed?
  - Has the council met its duty to have sufficient placements? Is there any possibility that, in an attempt to place children within the authority, the needs of children requiring more specialist provision are not being well met?
  - Is there effective multi-agency working to identify and tackle predatory adults within the community?

Scenario 2: Assessment and care planning

Concern

Jennifer is 12 months old. Her mother, Becky, is an 18-year-old care-leaver who came into care when her relationship with her mother broke down at age 14. A child protection conference was held soon after Jennifer's birth because of concern that Becky's drinking and drug use were causing her to neglect the baby, and Jennifer was made the subject of a child protection plan.

Over the next few months there were periods of stability interspersed with crises, and a couple of incidents when Jennifer was left alone in the flat. It was a particularly difficult time in the team and Jennifer had four different social workers before the age of 10 months.

At this point the local authority issued care proceedings and Jennifer was placed with foster family A, but then moved with Becky to a mother and baby residential assessment unit. This failed after a couple of weeks and Jennifer is now with foster family B. The court has asked the social worker to assess the capacity of the extended family and the birth father to care for Jennifer.

Additional information

- **A recent Ofsted inspection** criticised the council for its weak assessments in safeguarding cases.
- **Jennifer's guardian**, appointed by Cafcass, is questioning why Becky was not offered support from the local Sure Start service and Family–Nurse partnership scheme.
- **Becky's leaving care worker** is questioning whether care-leavers are subject to discrimination by assuming they will have difficulties in parenting their own children.

Action

Jennifer's maternal grandmother has been to see her local councillor (a member of the corporate parenting group) and is asking the following questions.

- Why has she not been contacted before when problems were first raised?
- Why has Jennifer had so many changes of social worker as she believes this has led to lost information about the family and the help they can offer?
- Why has Jennifer been cared for by so many different people?
- What damage has been caused to Jennifer by all these moves and changes of social worker?
- Why is it only now that Jennifer's father is being sought?

In response to the councillor's enquiry, the DCS has responded that Becky's own mother has problems coping and they feel it is in Jennifer's best interests to be adopted outside the family, which could take many months. They do not think it is appropriate to assess Jennifer's father because he is also involved in substance misuse. The DCS does acknowledge that it has been a difficult time within the social work team and there are problems in recruiting skilled staff.

Task

Consider how the Lead Member could arrive at a judgement about:

1. whether the standard of care is good enough for this child.
2. whether it raises wider issues about policy and practice in the authority.
3. what action might need to be taken.

Scenario 2: Assessment and care planning key points

In terms of Jennifer herself:

- How far were the changes of placement avoidable?
- What was the communication between the 16+/leaving care team social workers and Jennifer's social workers?
- Were appropriate services offered to Becky so that she was given every chance to care for Jennifer?
- Is the IRO in support of the plans for Jennifer?

Ultimately, the court will make decisions and must be satisfied that Jennifer would suffer significant harm if she remains in Becky's care. There are, however, wider implications for policy and practice:

- Are assumptions being made that someone with a history of care – or who is a substance misuser – will automatically be a poor parent?
- How does the council minimise disruption when making placement decisions, for example by retaining fostering placements if a child is likely to return to care?
- Are there sufficient foster carers to enable continuity and stability of care, and if not, how is the local authority addressing this?
- Has the council considered adopting a concurrent planning model for babies?
- How well does the council perform on the stability of placements and do babies have more or fewer moves than other age groups?
- What is the policy about involving family members – for example is there a 'family group conference' model?
- What has the council done to support the recruitment and retention of skilled social workers?
- What drug treatment services are available to looked after children/care-leavers and what priority do they have?

Determining priorities

The tasks for those responsible for driving improvements in corporate parenting can be overwhelming. The gap between the council's aspirations for its children and the reality of their experiences and outcomes may be considerable, and the challenge when determining a strategic plan is how to decide what is most important, and what can wait. It can be useful to identify some 'quick wins' so that positive changes can be achieved – and celebrated – relatively quickly.

There are several factors and interests that need to be balanced when determining what action to take. A pressing issue for one group of children may be irrelevant to others, and decisions need to involve a range of stakeholders.

The sources of evidence that should be used to inform forward planning include the following.

- **Profile of looked after children and care-leavers.** It is important to have a picture of who the council is caring for, including their age, gender, ethnicity and specific needs, in order to plan. There may be particular groups of children who are over or under-represented, or who have complex needs that may be difficult to meet within existing services.
- **Performance data.** Is the council performing particularly badly in relation to one set of outcomes, such as educational attainment or placement for adoption? If so, and there is evidence that there is a trend in that direction, specific measures may be needed to address the problem.
- **Children's experiences.** Statistical data should not be seen in isolation from qualitative information gathered from people on the receiving end of services. For example, a council may be performing well in relation to the timeliness of its health assessments, but if the children find their medicals to be an embarrassing and unhelpful experience, something needs to change. This evidence may be gathered directly through the Children in Care Council and an analysis of complaints, or indirectly through feedback from staff and carers.
- **Findings from scrutiny, inspection and quality assurance processes.** Deficiencies in the service may be highlighted by those with a scrutiny role. This could be external inspectors, scrutiny committees or officers with a quality assurance role such as Independent Reviewing Officers.
- **Stakeholder views.** There will be a range of views among staff, carers, looked after children and care-leavers about what their burning issues are. If they are to 'own' the council's strategy for looked after children, they should be given an opportunity to contribute to its development and to receive feedback about what was decided and why.
- **New research findings.** New evidence about the experiences and outcomes for looked after children may suggest changes in the way services are provided. For example, recent research about the increased risk of re-abuse for children who are rehabilitated home after a period in care should lead to increased vigilance in these circumstances.
- **Government policy.** At times, central government will decide to prioritise a particular aspect of the service, such as the number of children being adopted from care and the timeliness of their placement.

If you want to know more

Where to find more information

Every local authority approaches the corporate parenting task in a different way, and people are keen to learn from each other. There are a number of ways that people can find out what is happening elsewhere, to gain ideas for initiatives that may work for them or to engage with opportunities for peer support.

Local Government Association

The LGA is a cross-party membership organisation providing a number of resources, activities and events specifically designed to support local authorities. Their services include acting as a:

- knowledge hub to enable local authorities to connect and share information online. https://knowledgehub.local.gov.uk/
- 'peer challenge' programme, supporting local authorities to challenge and learn from each other. http://www.local.gov.uk/peer-challenge

Office for Standards in Education, Children's Services and Skills (Ofsted)

Ofsted inspects children's services. The framework from 2013 will jointly consider each council's services for looked after children, fostering and adoption, and how these operate together. In a separate programme, Ofsted will also consider local services for protecting children. The previous programme considered safeguarding and looked after services together and all the individual local authority reports are now available on the Ofsted website. This is a useful source of information for councils wishing to compare their effectiveness with that of others. http://www.ofsted.gov.uk/inspection-reports/find-inspection-report

Ofsted also conducts thematic inspections, such as one currently being undertaken on the role of the Independent Reviewing Officer in local authorities. http://www.ofsted.gov.uk/

Ofsted hosts the Children's Rights Director, although it is proposed this function will shortly be transferring to the Office of the Children's Commissioner. The Children's Rights Director for England consults children living away from home in regulated settings and represents their views in regular reports. For example, children have commented on their views of corporate parents. www.rights4me.org

There is also a young person's guide to good corporate parents. https://www.rights4me.org/~/media/Library%20Documents/Guides/GUIDE%20Young%20 Peoples%20Guide%20to%20Good%20Corporate%20Parents.pdf

Finally, Ofsted provides examples of good practice.
http://www.ofsted.gov.uk/resources/goodpractice

http://www.ofsted.gov.uk/resources/good-practice-resource-developing-effective-corporate-parenting-london-borough-of-lambeth

Centre for Excellence and Outcomes in Children's and Young People's Services

C4EO provides a range of products and support services to improve children's outcomes. Of particular interest to corporate parents will be the Centre's research reviews of services for looked after children and care leavers.
http://www.c4eo.org.uk/themes/vulnerablechildren/default.aspx?themeid=3&accesstypeid=1

Examples of validated and promising practice are also provided.
http://www.c4eo.org.uk/themes/general/localpracticeexamples.aspx?themeid=10

C4EO can assist local authorities by providing peer support through a network of sector specialists.

The Centre for Public Scrutiny

CFPS is a charity whose principal focus is on scrutiny, accountability and good governance, both in the public sector and among those people and organisations who deliver publicly funded services. It presents examples of local authority scrutiny reports, including some on services for looked after children, and also runs a Leadership Development Programme.
http://www.cfps.org.uk/

National Care Advisory Service

NCAS offers a range of resources focused on supporting looked after children to make the transition to adult life. This includes a helpline for young people and those working with them, publications and training and consultancy. NCAS also runs the 'From Care2Work' project, supporting young people into employment.
http://leavingcare.org/home

A National Voice

ANV provides a voice for children who are, or who have been, in care. It is run by people with care experience and offers a number of resources, training and consultancy services.
http://www.anationalvoice.org

Voice

Voice is a voluntary sector organisation aiming to empower children and young people, especially those in care. It provides an advocacy and independent visiting service, consultancy and training. It also hosts the Alliance for Child-Centred Care.
http://www.voiceyp.org/

The Who Cares? Trust

This trust acts as a voice and champion for looked after children, and includes on its website ideas for improving practice.
http://www.thewhocarestrust.org.uk/

Local authority websites

These are increasingly transparent in posting details of their work online. Many contain details of their corporate parenting strategy and governance arrangements, their Care Pledge and performance data.

The Department for Education

The DfE publish research summaries as well as information about the latest policy initiatives relevant to looked after children.
http://www.education.gov.uk/childrenandyoungpeople/families/childrenincare

The DfE has also produced resources for those commissioning children's services.
http://www.education.gov.uk/childrenandyoungpeople/strategy/b0072465/commissioning

Adoption and permanence: topic briefing

What are local authorities responsible for?

The current government is concerned that not enough children in care are being placed for adoption, and that the process is too slow. Their *Action Plan for Adoption* (DfE 2011) aims to tackle this and local authorities will be held to account for their performance.

When a child becomes looked after, the local authority must devise a care plan, setting out the objectives for the child and how these will be achieved. Once the child has been looked after for four months, this should include a plan for securing a permanent home where the child will be looked after for the rest of their childhood. There are several ways in which this can be achieved. For some children, the aim will be to resolve the family problems that led to their becoming looked after and to return them to the care of birth parents. For other children, it may be decided that this is not a safe option and alternative permanent carers must be found. Wherever possible, other family members or people with whom the child already has emotional ties would be the first option, and there is a statutory expectation that the local authority will explore this. These arrangements are usually known as 'kinship care', and there are a variety of legal ways in which the placement can be secured, such as residence orders, special guardianship or long-term fostering, as well as adoption. If there is no one suitable, then adoption by people unknown to the child may be considered.

Local authorities are responsible for devising the plan that will best meet the child's needs and putting it into place as soon as possible. They have been criticised for giving birth parents too many chances to improve their parenting skills with a view to resuming care of the children or being too slow to find permanent carers, either because of bureaucracy or because they are looking for the 'perfect' match.

Implications for corporate parents

The focus on adoption means that corporate parents should be aware of their own council's performance, not only in adoption but in securing permanence for looked after children. Data such as the profile of a child being adopted, timescales for moving them to adoptive placements once the decision has been made, and for responding to prospective adopters when they express an interest, are all important. Detailed data is now being collected and published by the Department for Education via 'adoption scorecards' that will allow local authorities to compare their performance with others. The government has made it clear what the minimum expectations are in terms of reducing delay.

As with all other aspects of the service, statistics only tell part of the story. Because numbers are likely to be relatively small, percentages can be misleading. It is important to know not only how many children are being placed but whether you are getting the adoptive placements right. Where adoptions break down, the effects on the individuals concerned can be devastating. Corporate parents will need to have information from officers about the story behind the statistics so that they can identify the measures that will improve outcomes.

Children will also have something to say. For young children adoption can give them the sense of belonging to a family that they need, but it is a radical option. It effectively provides a new family for the child, and some older children do not want to take this step. They would prefer a placement where they retain their family identity, while receiving long-term love and support in, for example, a permanent foster family.

Key guidance

Adoption statutory guidance: The Adoption and Children Act 2002
Department for Education (2012) *Statutory Guidance on Adoption*. Available at: http://media.education.gov.uk/assets/files/pdf/a/statutory%20guidance.pdf (accessed 17 January 2013).

Department for Education (2011) *An Action Plan for Adoption: Tackling Delay*. Available at: http://media.education.gov.uk/assets/files/pdf/a/an%20action%20plan%20for%20adoption.pdf (accessed 17 January 2013).

Other references/sources of information

DfE data on local authorities performance – 'adoption scorecards'
Department for Education (2012) Adoption Scorecards. Available at: http://www.education.gov.uk/childrenandyoungpeople/families/adoption/a00208817/adoption-scorecards (accessed 17 January 2013).

Ofsted data on the numbers and profile of adopters
Ofsted (2012) *Adoption Quality Assurance and Data Forms 2011–12: First Statistical Release*. Available at: http://www.ofsted.gov.uk/resources/adoption-quality-assurance-and-data-forms-2011-12-first-statistical-release (accessed 17 January 2013).

The British Association for Adoption and Fostering is a voluntary sector organisation that is a good source of information about good practice.
http://www.baaf.org.uk/

The Fostering Information Exchange is an online group on the Local Government Association's Knowledge Hub that allows users to create connections to peers and experts in the field of fostering.
http://www.baaf.org.uk/info/Fostering-Information-Exchange

Assessment, care planning and reviews: topic briefing

Every looked after child, whether they are subject to a care order, voluntarily accommodated or remanded into care, should have a care plan.

What are local authorities responsible for?

The care plan is the key individual planning tool for every looked after child. It sets out what the council intends for the child in the long term as well as the ways in which this will be achieved, and it includes a personal education plan and health plan. The care plan must be based on an assessment of the child's needs and regularly updated to reflect changing circumstances. Individual care plans must aim to deliver permanence and stability for the child and, through the provision of services, address difficulties arising from the child's history, development or disability. They should clearly identify who is responsible for taking action and timescales. Each looked after child must have a permanence plan within four months of becoming looked after.

Care plans are reviewed regularly and Independent Reviewing Officers (IROs) are responsible for ensuring that the care plan meets the needs of the child and that his or her views and wishes are considered. IROs are also responsible for monitoring the case between reviews and have a duty to challenge the council when a child's individual needs are not being met and when his or her human rights may be being breached.

Once a child reaches the age of 16 they should have a pathway plan, based on the previous care plan but setting out how they will be supported to achieve independence.

The placement plan sets out the contribution that the child's carers will make towards implementing the care plan, including their day-to-day responsibilities and their delegated authority to make decisions. The social worker and placement provider are responsible for drawing up this plan at the start of the placement and updating it as necessary.

Implications for corporate parents

Corporate parents must be satisfied that all children have an up-to-date care plan that is reviewed regularly and on time, and that plans are delivered taking into account the child's developmental timescales. Corporate parents should pay particular attention to how long a baby or very young child waits for a permanent placement, whether this is adoption, special guardianship or return home.

Sources of information that corporate parents can draw on include:

- **IRO report.** The IRO Service should produce an annual report for the corporate parenting group or equivalent. Corporate parents should consider what action is needed to remedy any problems identified.
- **Ofsted inspections.** The new framework for inspecting services for looked after children will focus more on the quality of individual care plans. Inspections will also look at the way the plans are used to inform strategic planning.
- **Local authorities** should have a system to monitor and audit the quality of their own care plans, and provide regular reports to the corporate parenting group.

When collated, care plans provide vital information about the overall needs that the authority and its partner agencies must address, and therefore the services that should be provided. This information should feed into the strategic plans of the authority and its partner agencies.

Key guidance documents

The Children Act 1989 guidance and regulations on care planning, placement and case review
Department for Children, Schools and Families (2010) *The Children Act 1989 Guidance and Regulations Volume 2: Care Planning, Placement and Case Review.* Available at:
https://www.education.gov.uk/publications/eOrderingDownload/DCSF-00185-2010.pdf (accessed 17 January 2013).

IRO Handbook: statutory guidance for Independent Reviewing Officers and local authorities on case management and review for looked after children
Department for Children, Schools and Families (2010) *IRO Handbook: Statutory Guidance for Independent Reviewing Officers and Local Authorities on their Functions in Relation to Case Management and Review for Looked After Children.* Available at:
https://www.education.gov.uk/publications/eOrderingDownload/DCSF-00184-2010.pdf (accessed 17 January 2013).

Short breaks – statutory guidance on how to use short breaks to safeguard and promote the welfare of disabled children
Department for Children, Schools and Families (2010) *Short Breaks: Statutory Guidance on How to Safeguard and Promote the Welfare of Disabled Children Using Short Breaks.* Available at:
https://www.education.gov.uk/publications/eOrderingDownload/short%20breaks%20 statutory%20guidance%20march%202010.pdf (accessed 17 January 2013).

The Children Act 1989 guidance and regulations on planning transitions to adulthood for care-leavers
Department for Children, Schools and Families (2010) *The Children Act 1989 Guidance and Regulations Volume 3: Planning Transition to Adulthood for Care Leavers.* Available at:
http://media.education.gov.uk/assets/files/pdf/v/volume%203%20planning%20transition%20 to%20adulthood%20for%20care%20leavers.pdf (accessed 17 January 2013).

Sufficiency – guidance on providing sufficient accommodation for looked after children
Department for Children, Schools and Families (2010) *Sufficiency: Statutory Guidance on Securing Sufficient Accommodation for Looked After Children.* Available at:
http://media.education.gov.uk/assets/files/pdf/s/statutory%20guidance%20securing%20 sufficient%20accommodation%20for%20looked%20after%20children%20march%202010.pdf (accessed 17 January 2013).

The Children Act 1989 guidance and regulations on local authority responsibilities towards former looked after children in custody
Department for Education (2010) *The Children Act 1989 Guidance and Regulations: Local Authority Responsibilities Towards Former Looked After Children in Custody.* Available at:
https://www.education.gov.uk/publications/eOrderingDownload/DfE-00562-2010.pdf (accessed 17 January 2013).

Other sources of information/good practice

Fostering Network report and tools to help social workers and fostering agencies to clarify foster carers' delegated authority
Fostering Network (2009) *Like Everyone Else: Full Report Of The Delegated Authority Project.* Available at:
http://www.fostering.net/delegated-authority (accessed 17 January 2013).

Children in Care Councils: topic briefing

What are local authorities responsible for?

Children in Care Councils (CiCCs) were introduced under the 'Care Matters' white paper guidance in 2007 and the present coalition government has continued to expect that each local authority will establish a CiCC and arrangements to support its operation. CiCCs should provide a child's view of how services for looked after children are working in practice, and as such should contribute to the monitoring functions of the corporate parent.

A mapping exercise undertaken by A National Voice (2011) found that a CiCC has been established in nearly all local authorities (although some have chosen to adopt a different name) but that they vary in the way they operate.

CiCCs should be encouraged to express the views of looked after children – and should receive feedback about the matters they raise. Issues raised by the CiCC should not relate to individual cases: they are not a substitute for the local authority's complaints procedure. Corporate parents should, however, be made aware of the types of complaint that are being raised and the steps that have been taken to resolve them. CiCCs should be enabled to contribute to the development of services and be consulted about strategic plans.

Implications for corporate parents

The CiCC is a valuable source of information for corporate parents. It can act as a useful counterbalance to the more formal reports that corporate parents receive. No matter what the data says, if the children on the receiving end of a service do not think it is good enough then corporate parents should respond.

Whatever the mechanism, there should be strong links between the CiCC and the corporate parent. Some CiCCs are represented through all the business of the corporate parenting group, others attend part of the group, or the corporate parenting group attends part of the CiCC's meetings by invitation. Consideration should be also given to matching the timing of meetings of the CiCC with those of the corporate parenting group and aligning agendas so that their respective activities fit together.

Corporate parents need to consider how best to support the CiCC to be effective. For example, how can the CiCC be enabled to represent *all* the authority's looked after children, including those who may be harder to reach.

Other ideas that may support the CiCC include:

- video telephone calls and conferencing
- newsletters
- participation workers employed to support the CiCC
- websites, social networking sites, and details of the CiCC contained in 'Welcome to Care' packs
- mechanisms for children in out-of-authority placements to contribute to the local CiCC
- events and activities to encourage involvement
- alternating the venues of CiCC meetings, especially in large, rural authorities
- providing the CiCC with its own budget, constitution and clear reporting lines to the corporate parenting group and full council
- a commitment by officers and members to attend CiCCs if invited to do so
- close involvement of the Director of Children's Services and Lead Member for Children's Services.

Key guidance documents

Statutory guidance on the roles and responsibilities of DCSs and Lead Members

Department for Education (2012) *Statutory Guidance on the Roles and Responsibilities of the Director of Children's Services and the Lead Member for Children's Services*. Available at: https://www.education.gov.uk/publications/eOrderingDownload/statutory%20guidance%20 on%20the%20roles%20and%20responsibilities%20of%20the%20dcs%20and%20lmcs.pdf (accessed 17 January 2013).

Children's complaints and representations regulations

http://www.legislation.gov.uk/uksi/2006/1738/contents/made (accessed 17 January 2013).

Other sources of information/best practice

Getting the best from complaints

Department for Education and Skills (2006) *Getting the Best from Complaints: Social Care Complaints and Representations for Children, Young People and Others*. Available at: https://www.education.gov.uk/publications/eOrderingDownload/Getting%20the%20best%20 from%20complaints.pdf (accessed 17 January 2013).

CiCC mapping project 2010–11

A National Voice (2011) *CiCC Mapping Project 2010–11: CiCCs across England – Mapping Performance and Function – Report by ANV for DfE*. Available at: http://media.education.gov.uk/assets/files/pdf/c/cicc%20mapping%20project%20november%20 2011.pdf (accessed 17 January 2013).

Ten points for CiCCs to monitor

Children's Rights Director (2012) *Ten-Point Guide on Issues for Children in Care Council's (CiCCs) to Monitor*. Available at: https://www.rights4me.org/~/media/Library%20Documents/Guides/GUIDE%20Ten%20Points%20 for%20CiCCs%20to%20Monitor.pdf (accessed 17 January 2013).

Young people's guide to good corporate parents

Children's Rights Director (2012) *Young Persons' Guide to Good Corporate Parents*. Available at: https://www.rights4me.org/en/home/library/guides/guide-young-persons-guide-to-good-corporate-parents.aspx (accessed 17 January 2013).

Children missing from care and sexual exploitation: topic briefing

There has been particular concern recently about children who go missing from care because of the serious harm that may ensue. Looked after children are particularly vulnerable to abuse and exploitation, and may also be at increased risk of placing themselves in danger from others or of self-harm.

An All Party Parliamentary Group enquiry into missing and runaway children from within the care system reported in June 2012 and made a number of recommendations relevant to local policy-makers.

Closely related to the issue of missing children is that of child sexual exploitation, and the government launched a National Action Plan in November 2011. A report has been published by the Office for the Children's Commissioner focusing on the specific issues for looked after children. The Local Government Association has also produced resources designed for elected members on this topic.

What are the local authority responsible for?

The Department for Education has produced guidance for local authorities on children missing from care. Local authorities must analyse incidents where children have gone missing from care and take action, particularly if there are recurring patterns that raise concern about certain placements. The objective must be to reduce the incidence of children going missing from care with a view to safeguarding and promoting their welfare. Ofsted will also need to see these reports when inspecting the local authority.

All children who are reported missing from care must be interviewed following each incident to ascertain the reasons and to plan how to protect them in the future. This interview should be undertaken by someone independent in case there are problems with the placement that the child wants to talk about. The IRO should be informed and should consider whether to bring forward the date of the next looked after child review. If a child is repeatedly going missing, the care plan and placement may not be suitable.

Children who are not in the care system are also at risk of going missing and the Local Safeguarding Children's Board (LSCB) has a responsibility towards them. Sexual predators may target both looked after children and vulnerable children living at home. Policies need to be aligned across agencies so that information is shared and there can be a concerted approach to keeping all children safe.

Implications for corporate parents

The corporate parenting group should be aware of the runaway and missing from home and care protocol in their authority and ensure that all agencies are signed up to and contribute to it. Any specific policies for looked after children need to reflect a council-wide approach led by the LSCB, which is responsible for protecting all children in the area.

Reports concerning missing from care incidents and responses should be considered by the corporate parenting group and used to make sure that services are being provided to support placements. The information might also point to gaps in the placements available, with a need to commission specialist protective resources for particularly vulnerable children. The lead senior manager responsible for missing from care monitoring and prevention strategies should present these reports.

Corporate parents need to be satisfied that action is being taken both to safeguard individual children missing from care and to address the problem at a strategic level.

Key guidance

DfE guidance on children missing from care
Department for Children, Schools and Families (2009) *Statutory Guidance on Children Who Run Away and Go Missing from Home or Care: Supporting Local Authorities to Meet the Requirements of National Indicator 71 – Missing from Home and Care*. Available at: https://www.education.gov.uk/publications/eOrderingDownload/DCSF-00670-2009.pdf (accessed 17 January 2013).

Child sexual exploitation action plan
Department for Education (2012) *Tackling Child Sexual Exploitation*. Available at: http://www.education.gov.uk/childrenandyoungpeople/safeguardingchildren/a00200288/tackling-child-sexual-exploitation (accessed 17 January 2013).

Other references/sources of information

Parliamentary report on children who go missing from care
APPG (2012) *The APPG for Runaway and Missing Children and Adults and the APPG for Looked After Children and Care Leavers Report From the Joint Inquiry into Children Who Go Missing From Care*. Available at: http://www.childrenssociety.org.uk/what-we-do/policy-and-lobbying/parliamentary-work/appg-inquiry-children-who-go-missing-or-run-away (accessed 17 January 2013).

Local government association resources on child sexual exploitation
http://www.local.gov.uk/safeguarding-children

Inquiry into child sexual exploitation in gangs and groups
Office of the Children's Commissioner for England (2012) *Briefing for the Rt Hon Michael Gove MP, Secretary of State for Education, on the Emerging Findings of the Office of the Children's Commissioner's Inquiry into Child Sexual Exploitation in Gangs and Groups, With a Special Focus on Children in Care*. Available at: http://www.childrenscommissioner.gov.uk/content/publications/content_580 (accessed 17 January 2013).

Child exploitation and online protection centre
http://ceop.police.uk/

Missing People, offering support and advice to parents/carers and missing people
http://www.missingpeople.org.uk/

Children's Society's '*Runaways Charter*' on how runaways should be treated
http://makerunawayssafe.org.uk/

Barnardo's research and campaigning on sexual exploitation
http://www.barnardos.org.uk/what_we_do/policy_research_unit/research_and_publications/sexual_exploitation_research_resources.htm

Children on the edge of care: topic briefing

What are local authorities responsible for?

Responsibility for looked after children cannot be seen in isolation from the council's responsibility towards all children in need within the area. Many children move in and out of the care system, perhaps at times of acute family stress. Others live with family or friends, rather than carers provided by the local authority, when parents cannot look after them safely. The care system needs to be part of an overall approach to supporting children, whatever their circumstances at the time. The term 'children on the edge of care' is used to refer to those whose family is at risk of breakdown or, conversely, where the child is being returned to the family following a period in care.

The Statutory Guidance on Sufficiency (DCSF 2010, para 1.8) describes the responsibilities of the local authority and its partners for such children. While the sufficiency duty applies to services for looked after children:

> ... an important mechanism – both in improving outcomes for children and in having sufficient accommodation to meet their needs – is to take earlier, preventive action to support children and their families so that fewer children become looked after. This means that the commissioning standard ... also applies to children in need who are at risk of care or custody (sometimes referred to as children 'on the edge of care').

(DCSF 2010, p. 4)

However, local authorities also need to bear in mind that research has shown that delaying entry into care for some children may be extremely costly both in terms of increased damage to the child's development, increasing difficulty in meeting their needs, delayed permanence and increased costs of placements.

> ... cutting back on early intervention and Section 17 family support services could increase the levels of maltreatment and its consequences especially if this is accompanied by attempts to reduce the numbers of children looked after away from home.

(Davies and Ward 2012, p. 90)

Also, the same research concerning children who have been returned home after a period or periods in care shows that outcomes for some of these children can be poor and they may not be safe.

> About two thirds of maltreated children who return home from care or accommodation are subsequently readmitted; this rises to 81% in the case of children whose parents are misusing drugs. Rates of readmission to care or accommodation should be carefully monitored and disseminated.

(Davies and Ward 2012, p. 91)

Implications for corporate parents

Corporate parents need to be wary of setting targets to reduce the numbers of children coming into care in their authority. Decisions should be driven by need, and the 'right' children should be coming into care at the 'right' time if outcomes are to improve.

Corporate parents should also be aware of the support needs of kinship carers and ensure that services are at least as good as those offered to foster carers. Kinship carers are often being asked to care for very damaged children and, in addition, they have to manage the complexity of relationships with birth parents.

Apart from children who are formally looked after, the local authority has a duty to visit children living in residential schools, hospitals or care homes for three months or longer. The duty requires the local authority to safeguard and promote their welfare and promote contact with their family and to see the child alone and write a report on the visit. A similar duty applies to children who were looked after on a voluntary basis if they enter custody through criminal justice legislation.

Corporate parents need to be aware of the different thresholds for intervention and to assure themselves that:

■ good family support services are available to prevent children from entering care unnecessarily

■ social work assessments are of high quality and able to identify children who cannot safely be cared for by their parents at any early stage and act quickly to provide alternative care

■ the right services are in place to address any problems that looked after children may have as soon as possible

■ children are only returned home from care where it is safe to do so, and ongoing support is offered to ensure the move has been successful

■ there are systems in place to fulfil the authority's responsibilities towards children in other placements away from home.

Key guidance

The 'sufficiency' duty, established in 2010 by the DCSF
Department for Children, Schools and Families (2010) *Sufficiency: Statutory Guidance on Securing Sufficient Accommodation for Looked After Children.* Available at:
http://media.education.gov.uk/assets/files/pdf/s/statutory%20guidance%20securing%20 sufficient%20accommodation%20for%20looked%20after%20children%20march%202010.pdf (accessed 17 January 2013).

Visits to Children in Long-Term Residential Care Regulations 2011
http://www.legislation.gov.uk/uksi/2011/1010/contents/made

Children Act 1989 guidance and regulations on local authority responsibilities towards former looked after children in custody
Department for Education (2010) *The Children Act 1989 Guidance and Regulations: Local Authority Responsibilities Towards Former Looked After Children in Custody.* Available at:
https://www.education.gov.uk/publications/eOrderingDownload/DfE-00562-2010.pdf (accessed 17 January 2013).

Other references/sources of information

Safeguarding children across services
Davies, C and Ward, H (2012) *Safeguarding Children Across Services: Messages from Research.* London: Jessica Kingsley Publishers. Available at:
https://www.education.gov.uk/publications/eOrderingDownload/DFE-RR164.pdf (accessed 17 January 2013).

Infants suffering harm
Ward, H, Brown, R, Westlake, D and Munro ER (2010) *Infants Suffering, or Likely to Suffer, Significant Harm: A Prospective Longitudinal Study.* London: Department for Education. Available at: http://www.lboro.ac.uk/research/ccfr/Publications/DFE-RB053.pdf (accessed 17 January 2013).

Maltreated children in the looked after system
Wade, J, Biehal, N, Farrelly, N and Sinclair, I (2010) *Maltreated Children in the Looked After System: A Comparison of Outcomes for Those Who Go Home and Those Who Do Not.* Research Brief, DFE-RBX-10-06. London: Department for Education. Available at: http://php.york.ac.uk/inst/spru/pubs/1786/ (accessed 17 January 2013).

Effective working with neglected children and their families
Farmer, E and Lutman, E (2012) *Effective Working with Neglected Children and their Families: Linking Interventions to Long-term Outcomes.* London: Jessica Kingsley Publishers.

Children who are at risk of offending and custody: topic briefing

What are local authorities responsible for?

Looked after children are more than twice as likely to enter the criminal justice system than their peers. They are also over-represented in the custodial population, as are care-leavers within adult prisons. The reasons for this are complex.

- Looked after children are more likely to have had adverse life experiences that increase their risk of offending behaviour.
- Inadequacies in the quality of care can increase these risk factors if, for example, children live in placements where there is poor supervision by adults or they are placed with older children who are already offending.
- There is evidence that some looked after children are 'criminalised' within the care system, with a lower threshold for prosecution than would be the case for children living at home.

The local authority should be aware of this increased risk, and make sure that individual care plans tackle any potential causes of offending. On a more general level, the local authority should make sure that the overall quality of care provision is not compounding children's emotional and behavioural difficulties, and that they are not 'criminalised' by an excessively punitive response.

The Children Act 1989 Guidance contains specific sections on looked after children and care-leavers, setting out what is expected of local authorities in relation to offending behaviour. These cover not only the prevention of offending but the need to offer continued support when children and young people are being dealt with by the criminal justice system, including custody.

Children in custody

The legal position of looked after children who go into custody is complex. Some children 'lose' their status as looked after children, some gain it and others remain the same. There are also new provisions under the Legal Aid, Sentencing and Punishment of Offenders Act 2012 that mean that, any child who is refused bail and remanded into a secure setting will become a looked after child. Any looked after child in custody is entitled to the same care planning and review as a child in care in the community.

Even where children 'lose' their looked after status in custody, the local authority has a duty to visit them and to assess their needs, including whether they will need to be looked after again on release. There is specific statutory guidance on this duty.

Implications for corporate parents

Corporate parents should be aware of the risks of children entering the criminal justice system and have plans in place to reduce them. They need to be aware of the numbers of looked after children who offend, including those who start offending when in care and those who started prior to becoming looked after; the type of offences and the risks they are exposed to; which groups of children are most vulnerable; and the services provided to prevent offending and to keep them safe and offence-free after a period in custody/at the end of their sentence.

Key guidance

Children Act 1989 guidance
Department for Children, Schools and Families (2010) *The Children Act 1989 Guidance and Regulations Volume 2: Care Planning, Placement and Case Review.* (Chapter 8 and Annex 5 describe local authority responsibilities to looked after children who offend.) Available at: https://www.education.gov.uk/publications/standard/Lookedafterchildren/Page1/DCSF-00185-2010 (accessed 14 January 2013).

Department for Children, Schools and Families (2010) *The Children Act 1989 Guidance and Regulations: Local Authority Responsibilities Towards Former Looked After Children in Custody.* Available at: https://www.education.gov.uk/publications/eOrderingDownload/DfE-00562-2010.pdf (accessed 17 January 2013).

Department for Children, Schools and Families (2010) *The Children Act 1989 Guidance and Regulations Volume 3: Planning Transition to Adulthood for Care Leavers.* Available at: https://www.education.gov.uk/publications/standard/Lookedafterchildren/Page1/DFE-00554-2010 (accessed 14 January 2013).

IRO Handbook
Department for Children, Schools and Families (2010) *IRO Handbook: Statutory Guidance for Independent Reviewing Officers and Local Authorities on their Functions in Relation to Case Management and Review for Looked After Children.* (Chapter 4 paras 4.9–4.12 are specifically concerned with children who offend.) Available at: https://www.education.gov.uk/publications/eOrderingDownload/DCSF-00184-2010.pdf (accessed 17 January 2013).

Other references/sources of information

Legal Aid, Sentencing and Punishment of Offenders Act 2012
Youth Justice Board (2012) *Implementation of the LASPO Act 2012: Key Stakeholder Information.* Available at: http://www.justice.gov.uk/youth-justice/courts-and-orders/legal-aid-sentencing-and-punishment-of-offenders-act-2012 (accessed 17 January 2013).

Views of children in care on care, offending and custody
Blades R, Hart, D, Lea, J and Willmott, N (2011) *Care: A Stepping Stone to Custody? The Views of Children in Care on the Links Between Care, Offending and Custody.* London: Prison Reform Trust. Available at: http://www.prisonreformtrust.org.uk/Portals/0/Documents/careasteppingstonetocustody.pdf (accessed 17 January 2013).

Looked after children and offending
Schofield G, Ward, E, Biggart, L, Scaife, V, Dodsworth, J, Larsson, B, Haynes, A and Stone, N (2012) *Looked After Children and Offending: Reducing Risk and Promoting Resilience.* Norwich: University of East Anglia. Available at: http://www.tactcare.org.uk/data/files/resources/52/lac_and_offending_reducing_risk_promoting_resilience_execsummary_080112.pdf (accessed 17 January 2013).

Education of looked after children: topic briefing

*Looked after children have a right to expect the outcomes we want for every child ...
local authorities as their 'corporate parents' should develop the strongest commitment
to helping every child they look after, wherever they are placed, to achieve the highest
educational standards he or she possibly can. This includes supporting their aspirations
to achieve in higher and further education.*

*Promoting the Educational Achievement of Looked After Children: Statutory Guidance
for Local Authorities*, (DCSF 2010, p. 3).

What are local authorities responsible for?

The gap between the educational attainment of looked after children and their peers has been a
long-standing cause for concern. *A Better Education for Children in Care* (Social Exclusion Unit
2003) identified five reasons why looked after children underachieve in education:

- their lives are characterised by instability
- they spend too much time out of school
- they do not have sufficient help with their education if they fall behind
- primary carers are not expected or equipped to provide sufficient support and
  encouragement for learning and development
- they have unmet emotional, mental and physical health needs which impact on their learning.

Although some of these reasons pre-date the child's entry to care, others are features of the care
system and can be avoided. When strenuous efforts are made, there is evidence that looked after
children can achieve educationally, and local authorities have a statutory duty to promote this
achievement, set out in the Children Act 1989 as amended by the Children Act 2004.

The government has issued specific statutory guidance on local authority duties to promote
achievement including the following.

1. **Education assessments and personal education plans**. Personal education plans (PEPs) must
   be completed for all children within 10 days of their becoming looked after and are part of
   the Care Plan. There is a joint responsibility for the PEP between the child's school and local
   authority children's service. Children with special educational needs will have an Individual
   Education Plan which should form part of the PEP.
2. **Priority for admission**. Looked after children have priority for admission to the schools that
   will best meet their needs, even if the school is full. This is set out in the Schools Admission
   code and applies to *all* maintained schools, including free schools and academies.
3. **Designated teachers**. Schools are required to have teachers who have specific responsibility
   for supporting looked after children.
4. **Protections against being moved or excluded from school**.
5. **Financial support**. Care-leavers are entitled to a bursary of £1,200 in further education and
   £2,000 if they go to higher education.

Although it is not yet mandatory (the Children and Families Bill may change that), most authorities
have created the post of a 'virtual school head' to co-ordinate the service to all the council's
looked after children, wherever they are placed. This enables the council to take an overview, and
provides the capacity to drive change at a senior level. Recent evaluations were positive about the
benefits of this role.

Implications for corporate parents

Corporate parents will need to receive regular reports on the attainment of their looked after children, but this must be balanced by information about the quality of children's experiences in school. The 'distance' travelled by children during their time in care may be more important than their test results. As well as attainment, information about whether children are being admitted to the 'best' schools, attendance and exclusions are an important part of the picture.

Key guidance

Promoting the Educational Achievement of Looked after Children
This statutory guidance sets out the detail of the measures that local authorities should take, including the specific responsibilities of the Lead Member for Children's Services and the Director of Children's Services.

Department for Children, Schools and Families (2010) *Promoting the Educational Achievement of Looked After Children: Statutory Guidance for Local Authorities*. Available at: https://www.education.gov.uk/publications/standard/publicationDetail/Page1/DCSF-00342-2010 (accessed 14 January 2013).

School Admissions Code
This describes the way that school governing bodies should give places to looked after children and those recently looked after.

Department for Education (2012) *School Admissions Code*. Available at: https://www.education.gov.uk/publications/standard/publicationDetail/Page1/DFE-00013-2012 (accessed 14 January 2013).

The role and responsibilities of the designated teacher for looked after children
Statutory guidance for school governing bodies.
Department for Children, Schools and Families (2009) *The Role and Responsibilities of the Designated Teacher for Looked After Children: Statutory Guidance for School Governing Bodies*. Available at:
https://www.education.gov.uk/publications/standard/publicationdetail/page1/DCSF-01046-2009 (accessed 17 January 2013).

The Bursary Fund Scheme
The scheme – contained in The Children Act 1989 (Higher Education Bursary) (England) Regulations 2009 – sets out the duty of local authorities to pay a bursary to all former relevant children who are undertaking a recognised course of higher education.
http://www.legislation.gov.uk/ukdsi/2009/9780111480663/contents (accessed 17 January 2013).

Other resources/sources of information

Education of looked after children FAQs
The DfE has produced answers to frequently asked questions on this topic.
Department for Education (2013) *Education of Looked after Children FAQs*. Available at:
http://www.education.gov.uk/childrenandyoungpeople/families/childrenincare/education/a0066445/education-of-looked-after-children-faqs (accessed 17 January 2013).

Virtual School Head Toolkit
The toolkit provides a range of materials to support virtual school heads, or equivalent, to fulfil their role.
Department for Children, Schools and Families (2010) *Virtual School Head Toolkit*. Available at: http://media.education.gov.uk/assets/files/pdf/v/virtual%20school%20head%20toolkit.pdf (accessed 17 January 2013).

Comparing educational attainments with national data
The DfE has produced a toolkit for local authorities to compare the educational attainments of their looked after children with national data and relate this to placement stability. It provides questions for corporate parents to ask in relation to its performance and services.
Department for Education (2012) *Raising the Aspirations and Educational Outcomes of Looked After Children: A Data Tool for Local Authorities*. Available at: http://www.education.gov.uk/childrenandyoungpeople/families/childrenincare/a00192332/raising-the-aspirations-and-educational-outcomes-of-looked-after-children-a-data-tool-for-local-authorities (accessed 17 January 2013).

The Booktrust Letterbox Club
The club provides books and other educational materials to looked after children aged 7–13.
http://www.letterboxclub.org.uk/about-us/ (accessed 17 January 2013).

Research evidence

Supporting young people not in education, employment or training
Nelson, J and O' Donnell, L (2011) *Approaches to Supporting Young People Not in Education, Employment or Training: A Review*. Slough: NFER. Available at: http://www.nfer.ac.uk/nfer/publications/RSRN01/RSRN01_home.cfm?publicationID=672&title=Approaches%20to%20supporting%20young%20people%20not%20in%20education,%20employment%20or%20training%20-%20a%20review (accessed 17 January 2013).

Evidence base for improving educational outcomes for looked after children
Summarised by C4EO.
Centre for Excellence and Outcomes in Children and Young People's Services (2012) *Improving the Educational Outcomes of Looked After Children and Young People (LACYP)*. Available at: http://www.c4eo.org.uk/themes/vulnerablechildren/educationaloutcomes/default.aspx?themeid=7 (accessed 17 January 2013).

Evaluation of the virtual school head pilot
Berridge, D, Henry, L, Jackson, S and Turney, D (2009) *Looked After and Learning: Evaluation of the Virtual School Head Pilot*. London: DCSF. Available at: http://media.education.gov.uk/assets/files/pdf/v/looked%20after%20and%20learning%20evaluation%20-%20virtual%20school%20head%20pilot.pdf (accessed 17 January 2013).

The impact of virtual schools
Ofsted examined the impact of virtual schools in nine local authorities.
Ofsted (2012) *The Impact of Virtual Schools on the Educational Progress of Looked After Children*. Available at: http://www.ofsted.gov.uk/resources/impact-of-virtual-schools-educational-progress-of-looked-after-children (accessed 17 January 2013).

Health of looked after children – including emotional and mental health: topic briefing

Children often enter the care system with a worse level of health than their peers, in part due to the impact of poverty, poor parenting, chaotic lifestyles and abuse or neglect. Longer term outcomes for looked after children remain worse than their peers.

Department for Children, Schools and Families (2009) *Statutory Guidance on Promoting the Health and Well-being of Looked After Children.*

What are local authorities responsible for?

As with education, looked after children are at risk of experiencing more problems than their peers, and the government has issued specific guidance setting out the statutory responsibilities of both the local authority and health agencies.

The government commissioned a review of children's problems before issuing the guidance, which found that high mental health needs are particularly prevalent, especially amongst children placed in residential care, but there were also a range of other physical and developmental problems.

Guidance states that health assessments should be carried out within four weeks of a child becoming looked after and then annually, except for children under the age of five, when it must be carried out every six months. The assessment should result in a health plan, which feeds in to the care plan. Local authorities are also required to ensure that a strengths and difficulties questionnaire (SDQ) is completed by the main carer for each looked after child aged 4–16 inclusive. This is a tool to assess for emotional and behavioural difficulties.

Health trusts are required to have designated doctors and nurses for looked after children, with a strategic role separate from the direct service they may offer to individual children. Different local areas operate different models but it is important that, whichever model is used, arrangements are in place to enable the designated professionals to have an impact on the commissioning of health services for looked after children.

Under the guidance, the roles of the NHS were set out. The NHS is responsible for commissioning effective services and providing coordinated care for each child, led by primary care trusts (PCTs) and strategic health authorities (SHAs). With the new health arrangements, whereby PCTs are abolished and replaced by Clinical Commissioning Groups (CCGs) of GPs, local arrangements will need to be made to ensure that the health of looked after children continues to be promoted. This is likely to be complex because the geographic boundaries of CCGs will not be co-terminous with those of local authorities. The NHS Commissioning Board has issued interim advice on how this might work but Directors of Public Health within local authorities will have a role in establishing local arrangements.

The Joint Strategic Needs Assessment (JSNA) and Joint Health and Wellbeing Strategy (JHWS) are the processes for identifying the current and future health and well-being needs of a local population, and leading to agreed commissioning priorities that will improve outcomes and reduce health inequalities. The Department of Health has issued guidance on how this will work.

Implications for corporate parents

Nationally, there has been increasing adherence to statutory timescales but this should continue to be monitored by corporate parents. They should also make sure that health providers allocate sufficient resources to meet the needs of looked after children. This includes direct health services, including child and adolescent mental health services (CAMHS), but should also ensure that looked after children's nurses and doctors have sufficient time to carry out sometimes complex assessments and can provide follow-up services to assist their health colleagues in meeting the children's needs.

Timescales are important but it is also vital to get feedback from children and young people about the quality of their experiences. Do they feel that their health assessments are user-friendly and of benefit to them? And are the health needs that are identified collated to inform the commissioning of services?

Key guidance

Government guidance for both social care and health agencies
Department for Children, Schools and Families (2009) *Statutory Guidance on Promoting the Health and Well-being of Looked After Children*. Available at: https://www.education.gov.uk/publications/standard/Healthanddisabilities/Page1/DCSF-01071-2009 (accessed 14 January 2013).

Rules about who is responsible for commissioning and paying for health services
Department of Health (2007) *Who Pays? Establishing the Responsible Commissioner*. Available at: http://www.dh.gov.uk/en/Publicationsandstatistics/Publications/PublicationsPolicyAndGuidance/DH_078466 (accessed 14 January 2013).

Guidance on the JSNA and JHWS processes
Department of Health (2010) *Joint Strategic Needs Assessment and Joint Health and Wellbeing Strategies Explained. Commissioning for Populations*. Available at: https://www.gpc.eoe.nhs.uk/page.php?page_id=395 (accessed 17 January 2013).

Department of Health (2012) *Consultation on Joint Strategic Needs Assessments and Joint Health and Wellbeing Strategy Guidance*. Available at: http://www.dh.gov.uk/health/2012/07/consultation-jsna (accessed 17 January 2013).

NHS Commissioning Board advice on safeguarding in the reformed NHS
National Health Service Commissioning Board (2012) *Arrangements to Secure Children's and Adult Safeguarding in the Future NHS: The New Accountability and Assurance Framework – Interim Advice*. Available at: https://www.education.gov.uk/publications/eOrderingDownload/NHS-interim-safeguarding.pdf (accessed 17 January 2013).

NICE and SCIE joint guidance
National Institute for Health and Clinical Excellence (2010) *Promoting the Quality of Life of Looked After Children and Young People*. Available at: http://www.nice.org.uk/PH28 (accessed 17 January 2013).

National Institute for Health and Clinical Excellence (2010) *Looked-after Children and Young People: Full Guidance*. Available at: http://guidance.nice.org.uk/PH28/Guidance/pdf/English (accessed 17 January 2013).

References and sources of further information

Promoting health

Mooney, A, Statham, J, Monck, E and Chambers, H (2009) *Promoting the Health of Looked After Children: A Study to Inform Revision of the 2002 Guidance.* DCSF Research Report No: DCSF-RR125. Available at:
https://www.education.gov.uk/publications/standard/publicationDetail/Page1/DCSF-RR125 (accessed 17 January 2013).

Criteria and a self-assessment toolkit

This sets out the principles to help health services become young people friendly.
Department of Health (2011): *You're Welcome: Quality Criteria for Young People Friendly Health Services.* Available at:
http://www.dh.gov.uk/en/Publicationsandstatistics/Publications/PublicationsPolicyAndGuidance/DH_126813 (accessed 17 January 2013).

C4EO review of services for improving emotional and behavioural health

Centre for Excellence and Outcomes in Children and Young People's Service (2009) *Improving the Emotional and Behavioural Health of Looked After Children and Young People.* Available at:
http://www.c4eo.org.uk/themes/vulnerablechildren/emotionalbehavioural/default.aspx?themeid=8 (accessed 17 January 2013).

Leaving care and moving on: topic briefing

What are local authorities responsible for?

Young people cease to be looked after at the age of 18, although some looked after children may choose to leave care before this. However, the local authority continues to have responsibilities towards them until at least the age of 21 and possibly up to 25. These duties and responsibilities vary according to the circumstances of the young person and their length of time in care prior to the age of 16.

Within three months of their sixteenth birthday (or three months of becoming looked after if they are aged 16–18), each child must have a pathway plan, setting out how they will be supported in their transition to adulthood and based on a needs assessment and their care plan. The pathway plan should also include other plans, health, education and employment, as well as the transition plan for children with disabilities who are subject to a statement of educational need. Care-leavers are entitled to the support of a personal advisor through this transition.

Children who do leave care before the age of 18 are entitled to financial support from their local authority, as well as assistance with accommodation and a range of other practical and emotional help.

Young people who are also eligible for adult services remain entitled to leaving care support and these services should be delivered in tandem, with strong collaboration between the personal advisor for leaving care and the adult services social worker.

Care-leavers over 18 remain entitled to Housing Benefit/Income Support if they are studying full time in further education, including A level. They can claim this up to their twenty-first birthday and continue to receive it until the end of their course of study/academic year following their twenty-first birthday, whichever is earlier. Sixteen to 19 year olds in further education are also entitled to claim the 16–19 bursary, administered by the education provider, and local authorities must pay a bursary to young people engaged in a course of higher education.

Implications for corporate parents

Corporate parents must ensure that all eligible looked after young people and care-leavers over 16 have a pathway plan and that this is reviewed regularly. They must ensure that the local authority keeps in touch with care-leavers and that they receive all the support and allowances they are entitled to. This includes providing opportunities for catching up, whether this is in education or employment or within health services, including access to mental health services. As young people mature they may be more willing to engage in services they have previously refused. They should be enabled and encouraged to remain in stable placements if this is in their best interests beyond the age of 18 and provided with 'safety nets' as well as support when they try to live independently.

Corporate parents will need to examine the statistical data that is available on their care-leavers, supported by feedback from the young people themselves. Many Children in Care Councils involve care-leavers, enabling them to maintain a continuing relationship with the authority.

Key guidance

Local authority statutory duties
Department for Children, Schools and Families (2010) *The Children Act 1989 Guidance and Regulations Volume 3: Planning Transition to Adulthood for Care Leavers*. Available at: https://www.education.gov.uk/publications/standard/Lookedafterchildren/Page1/DFE-00554-2010 (accessed 14 January 2013).

Bursary scheme for young people aged 16 to 19 in education
Department for Education (2012) *The 16–19 Bursary Fund.* Available at:
http://www.education.gov.uk/childrenandyoungpeople/youngpeople/studentsupport/funding/
a00203061/16-19-bursaries (accessed 17 January 2013).

Scheme covering local authority duties to young people in higher education
Contained in the Children Act 1989 (Higher Education Bursary) (England) Regulations 2009.
http://www.legislation.gov.uk/uksi/2009/2274/contents/made (accessed 17 January 2013).

The government charter for care-leavers
Department for Education (2012) *Charter for Care-leavers.* Available at:
http://media.education.gov.uk/assets/files/pdf/c/cl%20charter%20final%2025%20oct%202012.
pdf (accessed 17 January 2013).

Other references/sources of information

Enquiries service
National Care Advisory Service (NCAS), supported by Catch 22, is the national advice, support and
development service focusing on young people's transition from care. They offer a free enquiries
service to young people in or leaving care and those who work with them.
http://leavingcare.org/?page_ID=13#Home (accessed 17 January 2013).

Quality mark
Catch 22 NCAS 'From Care2Work' employers' quality mark. These opportunities may be offered 'in
house' or in partnership with local or national employers.
http://leavingcare.org/?page_ID=100019#From_Care2Work_Quality_Mark (accessed 17 January 2013).

Care-leavers' entitlements
Department for Education (2012) *Entitlements for Children in Care and Care Leavers.* Available at:
http://www.education.gov.uk/childrenandyoungpeople/families/childrenincare/a00208882/leavers
(accessed 15 January 2013).

Evidence base for supporting care-leavers into settled and secure accommodation
Centre for Excellence and Outcomes in Children and Young People's Services (2012) *Increasing the
Number of Care Leavers in 'Settled, Safe Accommodation'.* Available at:
http://www.c4eo.org.uk/themes/vulnerablechildren/careleavers/default.aspx?themeid=9 (accessed
17 January 2013).

Scheme supporting children staying in foster placements beyond the age of leaving care
Munro, ER, Lushey, C, Maskell-Graham, D and Ward, H with Holmes, L (2012) *Evaluation of the
Staying Put Pilots: 18 Plus Family Placement Programme.* Available at:
https://www.education.gov.uk/publications/RSG/publicationDetail/Page1/DFE-RR191 (accessed
17 January 2013).

Data pack supporting local authorities in examining their performance
Department for Education (2012) *Care Leavers Data Pack.* Available at:
http://www.education.gov.uk/childrenandyoungpeople/families/childrenincare/a00216209/
care-leavers-data-pack (accessed 17 January 2013).

'Access All Areas'
Catch22's National Care Advisory Service (NCAS), The Care Leavers' Foundation, A National Voice
and The Prince's Trust have launched the *Access all Areas* campaign, calling on central
government departments to 'care-proof' all their policies by assessing the impact they will have
on looked after children and care leavers and those who support them, with a specific focus on
young people aged 18–25.
http://www.catch-22.org.uk/News/Detail/Access-all-Areas-A-cross-departmental-government-
seminar-to-improve-journeys-from-care-to-adulthood (accessed 17 January 2013).

Regulation 33 visits: topic briefings

What are local authorities responsible for?

Local authorities that own, manage and run their own children's homes are required to appoint or identify personnel to undertake monthly visits to each home. These are known as Regulation 33 visits. They are quality assurance visits and should provide opportunities for officers or elected members carrying out these visits to assure themselves and others that they are providing the best quality care possible, that the children are safe and secure, their outcomes are good and they are encouraged to achieve.

Independent providers appoint their own visitors and reporting mechanisms.

The visits should cover:

- speaking to the children privately as a group or individually, with their consent
- speaking to staff as well as to parents or guardians of the children as appropriate
- inspecting the premises
- checking the complaints made
- checking the systems for running the home, especially behaviour management and records of any incident reports, restraint of children and details of incidents where children have been reported missing
- allegations of abuse within and outside the home and the risks the children are exposed to.

Visits can be announced or unannounced.

Who carries them out?

In many local authorities elected members carry out these visits and they provide a valuable opportunity to meet looked after children and directly assess the quality of care. In other authorities, officers carry out the visits, although they must be independent of the line management of the home. They can be also carried out jointly by an elected member and an officer, or a care-leaver could accompany them.

A balance should be struck between the people carrying out the visits being familiar to the children and therefore encouraging confidence and continuity, and also being able to offer objectivity and a fresh perspective.

A report of each visit should be written and these reports and the action taken should be considered by the corporate parenting group.

Implications for corporate parents

Corporate parents will need to decide how they will carry out the visits and the information that will come to the corporate parenting group. The Children in Care Council may have views on the best approach, and whether current arrangements are working. It is important that anyone undertaking Regulation 33 visits is properly trained so that they know how to talk to the staff and young people, including what *not* to say, and know what they are looking for. Training by care-experienced young people is likely to be particularly effective.

Consideration also needs to be given to the best format for the reports arising from the visits. Some reports get bogged down in recording minor maintenance issues rather than the bigger picture of whether the home is meeting the needs of the children placed there. It is also important that it is clear how any actions identified will be followed up and by whom. The corporate parenting group will also need to have a mechanism for making them aware of any trends, worrying incidents or safeguarding allegations within the homes they are responsible for. Ofsted inspections and rating should also be made available, so that all visits can take place with full information about the context.

Key guidance

Children's Homes Regulations 2001 (amended 2011)
http://media.education.gov.uk/assets/files/pdf/t/the%20childrens%20homes%20regulations%20 2001%20amended.pdf (accessed 17 January 2013).

Children Act 1989 guidance and regulations on children's homes
Department for Education (2011) *Children Act 1989 Guidance and Regulations Volume 5: Children's Homes*. (Paras 3.12 and 3.13 cover the detail of the visit.) Available at: https://www.education.gov.uk/publications/eOrderingDownload/DFE-00024-2011.pdf (accessed 17 January 2013).

Minimum standards for all homes
Department for Education (2011) *Children's Homes: National Minimum Standards 2011*. Available at:
https://www.education.gov.uk/publications/eOrderingDownload/NMS%20Children's%20Homes. pdf (accessed 17 January 2013).

Providers of residential special schools
Visits should be carried out once every half term.
Department for Education (2011) *Residential Special Schools: National Minimum Standards 2011*. Available at:
https://www.education.gov.uk/publications/eOrderingDownload/nms%20rss%20september%20 2011.pdf (accessed 17 January 2013).

Safeguarding: topic briefing

What are local authorities responsible for?

Local authorities must ensure that their children are protected from harm. This means that any risk of harm to individual looked after children must be assessed and plans put into place to keep the child safe. These risks include:

- physical and emotional harm
- sexual abuse and sexual exploitation
- bullying
- exposure to gangs/risk of harm from gangs
- self-harm and risk of suicide.

Such risks may come from family and friends, carers or the community. It could be that particular individuals from the child's network and placement are a risk to the child, or sectors of the community that target vulnerable children in care. The more isolated the child, the more vulnerable they may be to harm. Children who go missing from care are particularly at risk and there is a separate briefing on this, including the dangers of child sexual exploitation. Particular attention should be given to disabled and other children who may have difficulty communicating. All children should have someone they can communicate with, irrespective of their method of communication, and advocates and independent visitors should be used to make sure the child has someone outside the 'system' to look out for their interests.

Most children who have been subject to a child protection plan when living with their parents prior to coming into care will no longer need this intervention: being in care should keep them safe. However, if they are to return home consideration must be given to putting a child protection plan in place at that point. The decision to return a child home should always be linked to evidence that there has been sufficient change within the family, but evidence shows that such children are at particular risk (see the earlier briefing on 'Children on the Edge of Care').

Implications for corporate parents

Corporate parenting groups must link with the Local Safeguarding Children's Board (LSCB) and agree on the reports that each group receives concerning looked after children and those on the edge of care. Issues such as child sexual exploitation and children who go missing require a joint approach. Consideration within both groups should cover the particular risks that specific groups of looked after children are exposed to, including those placed out of authority, as well as the individual risks that individual looked after children present. The need to safeguard older teenagers and those within the youth justice system has often been underestimated, and corporate parents need to ensure that there are a broad range of suitable services.

All serious case reviews (SCRs) concerning looked after children and those on the edge of care, and any that have implications for policy and practice that may affect them, should be considered by corporate parenting groups. For example, an SCR may indicate that a decision to look after a child should have been made earlier and therefore corporate parenting groups may need to consider the threshold for care and how timely, evidence-based decisions are made.

Corporate parenting groups may want to consider having a thematic meeting on the safety of the council's looked after children, examining information such as:

- the risk of child sexual exploitation and the capacity of placements to protect children from it
- children placed in 'secure care' for their own welfare
- whether complaints of abuse have been made against staff or carers, and the outcome of investigations
- incidents of self-harm among older children, including those in custody
- 'trafficked' children and the provision to meet their needs.

Key guidance

Multi-agency guidance on the processes for safeguarding children
This is currently being updated.
Department for Children, Schools and Families (2010) *Working Together to Safeguard Children: A Guide to Inter-Agency Working to Safeguard and Promote the Welfare of Children.* Available at: https://www.education.gov.uk/publications/eOrderingDownload/00305-2010DOM-EN-v3.pdf (accessed 17 January 2013).

Statutory guidance including safeguarding needs
Department for Children, Schools and Families (2010) *The Children Act 1989 Guidance and Regulations Volume 2: Care Planning, Placement and Case Review* (paras 2.10–2.14). Available at: https://www.education.gov.uk/publications/standard/Lookedafterchildren/Page1/DCSF-00185-2010 (accessed 14 January 2013).

Child sexual exploitation
Department for Education (2012) *Tackling Child Sexual Exploitation.* Available at: http://www.education.gov.uk/childrenandyoungpeople/safeguardingchildren/a00200288/tackling-child-sexual-exploitation (accessed 17 January 2013).

Other references and sources of information

Safeguarding children who may have been trafficked
Department for Education (2011) *Safeguarding Children who May Have Been Trafficked: Practice Guidance.* Available at: https://consumption.education.gov.uk/publications/eOrderingDownload/DFE-00084-2011.pdf (accessed 17 January 2013).

Child Exploitation and Online Protection Centre
http://ceop.police.uk/ (accessed 17 January 2013).

Review of child protection arrangements
Professor Eileen Munro has undertaken a review of child protection arrangements and work is in progress to implement changes.
http://www.education.gov.uk/munroreview/ (accessed 17 January 2013).

Sufficiency duty: topic briefing

What are local authorities responsible for?

The statutory guidance on 'sufficiency':

> ... requires local authorities to take steps to secure so far as is reasonably practicable, sufficient accommodation within the authority's area which meets the needs of children that the local authority are looking after and whose circumstances are such that it would be consistent with their welfare for them to be provided with accommodation in the local authority's area.

(DCSF 2010: para 1.1)

In practice the duty can only be met through:

- partnership with other agencies carrying out their duty to cooperate to improve the well-being of children in the local area.
- commissioning services to meet needs, reduce placement breakdowns and to prevent children from becoming looked after unnecessarily.

Local authorities are required to demonstrate how they are meeting the requirements of the duty by drawing up plans and priorities for action. These need to be based on an analysis of needs, including those identified within individual care plans of looked after children and child in need plans.

Implications for corporate parents

Corporate parents should be aware of their council's plan to meet its sufficiency duty, and be satisfied that it is based on sound evidence. Where there appear to be gaps in provision, a strategic plan needs to be in place to address these. Measures could include targeted recruitment campaigns for foster carers, regional commissioning to meet complex and scarce needs, a review of the reasons people leave fostering and commissioning extra supports; an analysis of the needs of children who have had placement breakdowns; a review of children in out-of-authority placements and the reasons.

Key guidance

Statutory guidance on securing sufficient accommodation
Department for Children, Schools and Families (2010) *Sufficiency: Statutory Guidance on Securing Sufficient Accommodation for Looked After Children.* Available at:
http://media.education.gov.uk/assets/files/pdf/s/statutory%20guidance%20securing%20
sufficient%20accommodation%20for%20looked%20after%20children%20march%20
2010.pdf (accessed 17 January 2013).

Other references

Cost calculator
The Centre for Child and Family Research at Loughborough University has produced a cost calculator to support local authorities to analyse the true cost of services.
http://www.ccfcs.org.uk/ (accessed 17 January 2013).

Commissioning and paying for health services

The Department of Health has clarified the arrangements for commissioning and paying for health services.

Department of Health (2007) *Who Pays? Establishing the Responsible Commissioner.* Available at: http://www.dh.gov.uk/en/Publicationsandstatistics/Publications/PublicationsPolicyAndGuidance/ DH_078466 (accessed 14 January 2013).

Reform of children's homes

The government is currently consulting on the reform of children's homes.

https://www.education.gov.uk/childrenandyoungpeople/safeguardingchildren/a00213690/ childrens-residential-care-reform (accessed 14 January 2013).

Analysing performance

The DfE has provided a data pack to enable local authorities to analyse performance in relation to children's homes.

Department for Education (2012) *Children's Homes Data Pack.* Available at: http://www.education.gov.uk/childrenandyoungpeople/families/childrenincare/childrenshomes/ a00192000/childrens-homes-data-pack (accessed 17 January 2013).

Foster placements

Ofsted has produced data on the numbers and profile of foster placements.

Ofsted (2012) *Fostering Quality Assurance and Data Forms 2011–12 First Statistical Release.* Available at: http://www.ofsted.gov.uk/resources/fostering-quality-assurance-and-data-forms-2011-12-first- statistical-release (accessed 17 January 2013).

Ofsted (2012) *Press Release: A State of the Nation Picture on Adoption.* Available at: http://www.ofsted.gov.uk/news/state-of-nation-picture-adoption?news=19995 (accessed 17 January 2013).

Working in partnership to meet the needs of looked after children: topic briefing

What are local authorities responsible for?

Local authorities, on their own, will be unable to meet the sometimes complex needs of looked after children and, equally important, the needs of children on the edge of care and their families. Although local authorities have ultimate responsibility as 'corporate parents' for looked after children, they are entitled to the support of other agencies through their statutory duty to cooperate to safeguard and promote children's welfare.

Partnership arrangements need to be set up so that all agencies involved understand the needs of looked after children and children on the edge of care. These can be through Children's Trust arrangements, but it is at the discretion of each local authority area to set up the structures that will work best locally. The Joint Strategic Needs Assessment (JSNA) remains the key planning tool for local authorities and their partners to identify local needs, and it is important that looked after children and care-leavers are explicitly considered within that process. Looked after children's needs can get lost because they constitute a relatively small number of each area's population and the Director of Children's Services and the Lead Member for Children's Services should make sure this does not happen. The consequences of unmet needs are serious for children as this can affect their ability to learn, social skills and interaction, identity, their ability to gain employment and to fulfil their aspirations and, ultimately, to high and continuing costs in adulthood.

Implications for corporate parents

Individual elected members may sit on partnership boards, be a school governor or have other roles where they can influence services for looked after children. They should take every opportunity to make sure that they act as responsible corporate parents for looked after children and represent their best interests with a view to ensuring their needs are met, they are not treated differently and that their outcomes are good. This might involve arguing for targeted services, such as child mental team specialists for looked after children.

Whatever the local governance arrangements are for corporate parenting, they should involve representatives from the other agencies that are key to improving the outcomes of looked after children and care-leavers. These representatives should be sufficiently senior to be able to make decisions on behalf of their agency and to commit resources. Agencies that should be linked with the corporate parenting group in some way are the local NHS, education providers, housing providers, leisure services and criminal justice agencies. All of these agencies should be able to identify the ways in which their service is meeting the needs of looked after children and care-leavers and to feed into the council's corporate parenting strategy. For example, the local Youth Offending Team should be able to provide evidence on the numbers of looked after children that it is working with and the way it is working with children's social workers to reduce their risks. Housing providers should have a protocol for referring homeless 16 and 17 year olds to children's services to assess if they need to be accommodated, and to make provision for offering suitable housing to care-leavers. They should be able to provide evidence to the corporate parenting group about the numbers of children in these categories that they have helped, and their plans for future delivery.

As always, children will be able to describe their experiences of services provided by partner agencies so that corporate parents can identify where they need to exert influence to raise the standard.

Key guidance

Children Act 2004
The Children Act 2004 places a duty on all key agencies to cooperate to improve the well-being of children and young people (Section 10), and to ensure their functions are discharged with regard to the need to safeguard and promote the welfare of children (Section 11).
http://www.legislation.gov.uk/ukpga/2004/31/contents (accessed 17 January 2013).

Education Act 2002
The Education Act 2002 (Sections 157 and 175) places the same duties of cooperation to improve the well-being of children and to safeguard their welfare on schools and colleges of further education.
http://www.legislation.gov.uk/ukpga/2002/32/contents (accessed 17 January 2013).

Working together
The coalition government has described how it expects agencies to work together.
Department for Education (2012) *More Freedom and Flexibility: A New Approach for Children's Trust Boards*. Available at:
http://www.education.gov.uk/childrenandyoungpeople/healthandwellbeing/a00202982/anewapproachfor-childrenstrustboards (accessed 17 January 2013).

JSNAs and JHWSs
The Department of Health has consulted on draft guidance on a framework for NHS and local government to work together to undertake joint strategic needs assessments (JSNAs) and joint health and well-being strategies (JHWSs).
Department of Health (2012) *Consultation on Joint Strategic Needs Assessments and Joint Health and Wellbeing Strategy Guidance*. Available at:
http://www.dh.gov.uk/health/2012/07/consultation-jsna/ (accessed 17 January 2013).

Other references/sources of information

Local commissioning of services for children
DfE has produced resources to support local commissioning of services for children.
Department for Education (2012) *Commissioning*. Available at:
http://www.education.gov.uk/childrenandyoungpeople/strategy/b0072465/commissioning (accessed 17 January 2013).

Operating Framework
One of the key themes of the operating framework for the NHS is to put patients at the centre of decision making to achieve an outcomes approach to service delivery. This principle is at the heart of the changes envisaged for the NHS over the next few years and should continue beyond the life of this Operating Framework.
Department of Health (2012) *The Operating Framework for the NHS in England 2012/13*. Available at:
http://www.dh.gov.uk/prod_consum_dh/groups/dh_digitalassets/documents/digitalasset/dh_131428.pdf (accessed 17 January 2013).

Accountability and assurance framework
National Health Service Commissioning Board (2012) *Arrangements to Secure Children's and Adult Safeguarding in the Future NHS: The New Accountability and Assurance Framework – Interim Advice*. Available at:
https://www.education.gov.uk/publications/eOrderingDownload/NHS-interim-safeguarding.pdf (accessed 17 January 2013).

Bibliography

A National Voice (2011) *CiCC Mapping Project 2010–11: CiCCs across England – Mapping Performance and Function – Report by ANV for DfE.* Available at: http://media.education.gov. uk/assets/files/pdf/c/cicc%20mapping%20project%20november%202011.pdf (accessed 17 January 2013).

APPG (2012) *The APPG for Runaway and Missing Children and Adults and the APPG for Looked After Children and Care Leavers Report From the Joint Inquiry into Children who Go Missing from Care.* Available at: http://www.childrenssociety.org.uk/what-we-do/policy-and-lobbying/parliamentary-work/appg-inquiry-children-who-go-missing-or-run-away (accessed 17 January 2013).

Berridge, D, Henry, L, Jackson, S and Turney, D (2009) *Looked After and Learning: Evaluation of the Virtual School Head Pilot.* London: DSCF. Available at: http://media.education.gov.uk/assets/files/pdf/v/looked%20after%20and%20learning%20evaluation%20-%20virtual%20school%20head%20pilot.pdf (accessed 17 January 2013).

Blades, R, Hart, D, Lea, J and Willmott, N (2011) *Care: A Stepping Stone to Custody? The Views of Children in Care on the Links Between Care, Offending and Custody.* London: Prison Reform Trust. Available at: http://www.prisonreformtrust.org.uk/Portals/0/Documents/careasteppingstonetocustody.pdf (accessed 17 January 2013).

Centre for Excellence and Outcomes in Children and Young People's Service (2009) *Improving the Emotional and Behavioural Health of Looked After Children and Young People.* Available at: http://www.c4eo.org.uk/themes/vulnerablechildren/emotionalbehavioural/default.aspx?themeid=8 (accessed 17 January 2013).

Centre for Excellence and Outcomes in Children and Young People's Services (2012a) *Improving the Educational Outcomes of Looked After Children and Young People (LACYP).* Available at: http://www.c4eo.org.uk/themes/vulnerablechildren/educationaloutcomes/default.aspx?themeid=7 (accessed 17 January 2013).

Centre for Excellence and Outcomes in Children and Young People's Services (2012b) *Increasing the Number of Care Leavers in 'Settled, Safe Accommodation'.* Available at: http://www.c4eo.org.uk/themes/vulnerablechildren/careleavers/default.aspx?themeid=9 (accessed 17 January 2013).

Children's Rights Director (2011) *Having Corporate Parents: 'We're Not Treated Like Children, We're a Case'.* Available at: https://www.rights4me.org/home/library/reports/report-having-corporate-parents.aspx (accessed 15 January 2013).

Children's Rights Director (2012a) *Ten-Point Guide on Issues for Children in Care Council's (CiCCs) to Monitor.* Available at: https://www.rights4me.org/~/media/Library%20Documents/Guides/GUIDE%20Ten%20Points%20for%20CiCCs%20to%20Monitor.pdf (accessed 17 January 2013).

Children's Rights Director (2012b) *Young People's Guide to Good Corporate Parents.* Available at: https://www.rights4me.org/en/home/library/guides/guide-young-persons-guide-to-good-corporate-parents.aspx (accessed 15 January 2013).

Davies, C and Ward, H (2012) *Safeguarding Children Across Services: Messages from Research.* London: Jessica Kingsley Publishers. Available at: https://www.education.gov.uk/publications/eOrderingDownload/DFE-RR164.pdf (accessed 17 January 2013).

Department for Children, Schools and Families (2009a) *Statutory Guidance on Children Who Run Away and Go Missing from Home or Care: Supporting Local Authorities to Meet the Requirements of National Indicator 71 – Missing from Home and Care.* Available at: https://www.education.gov.uk/publications/eOrderingDownload/DCSF-00670-2009.pdf (accessed 17 January 2013).

Department for Children, Schools and Families (2009b) *Statutory Guidance on Promoting the Health and Well-being of Looked After Children*. Available at: https://www.education.gov.uk/publications/standard/Healthanddisabilities/Page1/DCSF-01071-2009 (accessed 14 January 2013).

Department for Children, Schools and Families (2009c) *The Role and Responsibilities of the Designated Teacher for Looked After Children: Statutory Guidance for School Governing Bodies*. Available at: https://www.education.gov.uk/publications/standard/publicationdetail/page1/DCSF-01046-2009 (accessed 17 January 2013).

Department for Children, Schools and Families (2010a) *IRO Handbook: Statutory Guidance for Independent Reviewing Officers and Local Authorities on their Functions in Relation to Case Management and Review for Looked After Children*. Available at: https://www.education.gov.uk/publications/eOrderingDownload/DCSF-00184-2010.pdf (accessed 17 January 2013).

Department for Children, Schools and Families (2010b) *Promoting the Educational Achievement of Looked After Children: Statutory Guidance for Local Authorities*. Available at: https://www.education.gov.uk/publications/standard/publicationDetail/Page1/DCSF-00342-2010 (accessed 14 January 2013).

Department for Children, Schools and Families (2010c) *Short Breaks: Statutory Guidance on How to Safeguard and Promote the Welfare of Disabled Children Using Short Breaks*. Available at: https://www.education.gov.uk/publications/eOrderingDownload/short%20breaks%20statutory%20guidance%20march%202010.pdf (accessed 17 January 2013).

Department for Children, Schools and Families (2010d) *Sufficiency: Statutory Guidance on Securing Sufficient Accommodation for Looked After Children*. Available at: http://media.education.gov.uk/assets/files/pdf/s/statutory%20guidance%20securing%20sufficient%20accommodation%20for%20looked%20after%20children%20march%202010.pdf (accessed 17 January 2013).

Department for Children, Schools and Families (2010e) *The Children Act 1989 Guidance and Regulations Volume 2: Care Planning, Placement and Case Review*. Available at: https://www.education.gov.uk/publications/standard/Lookedafterchildren/Page1/DCSF-00185-2010 (accessed 14 January 2013).

Department for Children, Schools and Families (2010f) *The Children Act 1989 Guidance and Regulations Volume 3: Planning Transition to Adulthood for Care Leavers*. Available at: https://www.education.gov.uk/publications/standard/Lookedafterchildren/Page1/DFE-00554-2010 (accessed 14 January 2013).

Department for Children, Schools and Families (2010g) *Virtual School Head Toolkit*. Available at: http://media.education.gov.uk/assets/files/pdf/v/virtual%20school%20head%20toolkit.pdf (accessed 17 January 2013).

Department for Children, Schools and Families (2010h) *Working Together to Safeguard Children: A Guide to Inter-Agency Working to Safeguard and Promote the Welfare of Children*. Available at: https://www.education.gov.uk/publications/eOrderingDownload/00305-2010DOM-EN-v3.pdf (accessed 17 January 2013).

Department for Education (2010) *The Children Act 1989 Guidance and Regulations: Local Authority Responsibilities Towards Former Looked After Children in Custody*. Available at: https://www.education.gov.uk/publications/eOrderingDownload/DfE-00562-2010.pdf (accessed 17 January 2013).

Department for Education (2011a) *An Action Plan for Adoption: Tackling Delay*. Available at: http://media.education.gov.uk/assets/files/pdf/a/an%20action%20plan%20for%20adoption.pdf (accessed 17 January 2013).

Department for Education (2011b) *Children Act 1989 Guidance and Regulations Volume 5: Children's Homes*. Available at: https://www.education.gov.uk/publications/eOrderingDownload/DFE-00024-2011.pdf (accessed 17 January 2013).

Department for Education (2011c) *Children's Homes: National Minimum Standards 2011*. Available at: https://www.education.gov.uk/publications/eOrderingDownload/NMS%20Children's%20Homes.pdf (accessed 17 January 2013).

Department for Education (2011d) *Outcomes for Children Looked After by Local Authorities in England: 12 Months to 30 September 2010 – Table 7.2.* Available at: http://www.education.gov.uk/researchandstatistics/datasets/a00200452/outcomes-for-children-looked-after-by-local-authorities-in-england-as-at-31-march-2011 (accessed 14 January 2013).

Department for Education (2011e) *Residential Special Schools: National Minimum Standards 2011.* Available at: https://www.education.gov.uk/publications/eOrderingDownload/nms%20rss%20september%202011.pdf (accessed 17 January 2013).

Department for Education (2011f) *Safeguarding Children who May Have Been Trafficked: Practice Guidance.* Available at: https://consumption.education.gov.uk/publications/eOrderingDownload/DFE-00084-2011.pdf (accessed 17 January 2013).

Department for Education (2012a) *Adoption Scorecards.* Available at: http://www.education.gov.uk/childrenandyoungpeople/families/adoption/a00208817/adoption-scorecards (accessed 17 January 2013).

Department for Education (2012b) *Care Leavers Data Pack.* Available at: http://www.education.gov.uk/childrenandyoungpeople/families/childrenincare/a00216209/care-leavers-data-pack (accessed 17 January 2013).

Department for Education (2012c) *Charter for Care-leavers.* Available at: http://media.education.gov.uk/assets/files/pdf/c/cl%20charter%20final%2025%20oct%202012.pdf (accessed 17 January 2013).

Department for Education (2012d) *Children Looked After in England: Year Ending March 2012.* Available at: http://www.education.gov.uk/researchandstatistics/statistics/a00213762/children-looked-after-las-england (accessed 14 January 2013).

Department for Education (2012e) *Children's Homes Data Pack.* Available at: http://www.education.gov.uk/childrenandyoungpeople/families/childrenincare/childrenshomes/a00192000/childrens-homes-data-pack (accessed 17 January 2013).

Department for Education (2012f) *Commissioning.* Available at: http://www.education.gov.uk/childrenandyoungpeople/strategy/b0072465/commissioning (accessed 17 January 2013).

Department for Education (2012g) *Entitlements for Children in Care and Care Leavers.* Available at: http://www.education.gov.uk/childrenandyoungpeople/families/childrenincare/a00208882/leavers (accessed 15 January 2013).

Department for Education (2012h) *More Freedom and Flexibility: A New Approach for Children's Trust Boards.* Available at: http://www.education.gov.uk/childrenandyoungpeople/healthandwellbeing/a00202982/anewapproachfor-childrenstrustboards (accessed 17 January 2013).

Department for Education (2012i) *Raising the Aspirations and Educational Outcomes of Looked After Children: A Data Tool for Local Authorities.* Available at: http://www.education.gov.uk/childrenandyoungpeople/families/childrenincare/a00192332/raising-the-aspirations-and-educational-outcomes-of-looked-after-children-a-data-tool-for-local-authorities (accessed 17 January 2013).

Department for Education (2012j) *School Admissions Code.* Available at: https://www.education.gov.uk/publications/standard/publicationDetail/Page1/DFE-00013-2012 (accessed 14 January 2013).

Department for Education (2012k) *Statutory Guidance on Adoption.* Available at: http://media.education.gov.uk/assets/files/pdf/a/statutory%20guidance.pdf (accessed 17 January 2013).

Department for Education (2012l) *Statutory Guidance on the Roles and Responsibilities of the Director Of Children's Services and the Lead Member for Children's Services.* Available at: https://www.education.gov.uk/publications/eOrderingDownload/statutory%20guidance%20on%20the%20roles%20and%20responsibilities%20of%20the%20dcs%20and%20lmcs.pdf (accessed 17 January 2013).

Department for Education (2012m) *Tackling Child Sexual Exploitation.* Available at: http://www.education.gov.uk/childrenandyoungpeople/safeguardingchildren/a00200288/tackling-child-sexual-exploitation (accessed 17 January 2013).

Department for Education (2012n) *The 16–19 Bursary Fund.* Available at: http://www.education. gov.uk/childrenandyoungpeople/youngpeople/studentsupport/funding/a00203061/16-19- bursaries (accessed 17 January 2013).

Department for Education (2013) *Education of Looked after Children FAQs.* Available at: http:// www.education.gov.uk/childrenandyoungpeople/families/childrenincare/education/ a0066445/education-of-looked-after-children-faqs (accessed 17 January 2013).

Department for Education and Skills (2006) *Getting the Best from Complaints: Social Care Complaints and Representations for Children, Young People and Others.* Available at: https:// www.education.gov.uk/publications/eOrderingDownload/Getting%20the%20best%20 from%20complaints.pdf (accessed 17 January 2013).

Department for Education and Skills (2007) *Care Matters: Time for Change.* Norwich: The Stationery Office.

Department of Health (2007) *Who Pays? Establishing the Responsible Commissioner.* Available at: http://www.dh.gov.uk/en/Publicationsandstatistics/Publications/ PublicationsPolicyAndGuidance/DH_078466 (accessed 14 January 2013).

Department of Health (2010) *Joint Strategic Needs Assessment and Joint Health and Wellbeing Strategies Explained Commissioning for Populations.* Available at: https://www.gpc.eoe.nhs. uk/page.php?page_id=395 (accessed 17 January 2013).

Department of Health (2011) *You're Welcome: Quality Criteria for Young People Friendly Health Services.* Available at: *http://www.dh.gov.uk/en/Publicationsandstatistics/Publications/ PublicationsPolicyAndGuidance/DH_126813* (accessed 17 January 2013).

Department of Health (2012a) *Consultation on Joint Strategic Needs Assessments and Joint Health and Wellbeing Strategy Guidance.* Available at: http://www.dh.gov.uk/health/2012/07/ consultation-jsna (accessed 17 January 2013).

Department of Health (2012b) *The Mandate: A Mandate from the Government to the NHS Commissioning Board – April 2013 to March 2015.* Available at: https://www.wp.dh.gov.uk/ publications/files/2012/11/mandate.pdf (accessed 14 January 2013).

Department of Health (2012c) *The Operating Framework for the NHS in England 2012/13.* Available at: http://www.dh.gov.uk/prod_consum_dh/groups/dh_digitalassets/documents/digitalasset/ dh_131428.pdf (accessed 17 January 2013).

Farmer, E and Lutman, E (2012) *Effective Working with Neglected Children and their Families: Linking Interventions to Long-term Outcomes.* London: Jessica Kingsley Publishers.

Fostering Network (2009) *Like Everyone Else: Full Report Of The Delegated Authority Project.* Available at: http://www.fostering.net/delegated-authority (accessed 17 January 2013).

Hart, D and Williams, A (2008) *Putting Corporate Parenting into Practice: Developing an Effective Approach.* London: National Children's Bureau.

Mooney, A, Statham, J, Monck, E and Chambers, H (2009) *Promoting the Health of Looked After Children: A Study to Inform Revision of the 2002 Guidance.* DCSF Research Report No: DCSF- RR125. Available at: https://www.education.gov.uk/publications/standard/ publicationDetail/Page1/DCSF-RR125 (accessed 17 January 2013).

Munro, ER, Lushey, C, Maskell-Graham, D and Ward, H with Holmes, L (2012) *Evaluation of the Staying Put Pilots: 18 Plus Family Placement Programme.* Available at: https://www.education.gov.uk/publications/RSG/publicationDetail/Page1/DFE-RR191 (accessed 17 January 2013).

National Health Service Commissioning Board (2012) *Arrangements to Secure Children's and Adult Safeguarding in the Future NHS: The New Accountability and Assurance Framework – Interim Advice.* Available at: https://www.education.gov.uk/publications/eOrderingDownload/ NHS-interim-safeguarding.pdf (accessed 17 January 2013).

National Institute for Health and Clinical Excellence (2010a) *Looked-after Children and Young People: Full Guidance.* Available at: http://guidance.nice.org.uk/PH28/Guidance/pdf/English (accessed 17 January 2013).

National Institute for Health and Clinical Excellence (2010b) *Promoting the Quality of Life of Looked After Children and Young People.* Available at: http://www.nice.org.uk/PH28 (accessed 17 January 2013).

Nelson, J and O' Donnell, L (2011) *Approaches to Supporting Young People Not in Education, Employment or Training: A Review.* Slough: NFER. Available at: http://www.nfer.ac.uk/nfer/publications/RSRN01/RSRN01_home.cfm?publicationID=672&title=Approaches%20to%20supporting%20young%20people%20not%20in%20education,%20employment%20or%20training%20-%20a%20review (accessed 17 January 2013).

Office of the Children's Commissioner for England (2012) *Briefing for the Rt Hon Michael Gove MP, Secretary of State for Education, on the Emerging Findings of the Office of the Children's Commissioner's Inquiry into Child Sexual Exploitation in Gangs and Groups, with a Special Focus on Children in Care.* Available at http://www.childrenscommissioner.gov.uk/content/publications/content_580 (accessed 14 January 2013).

Ofsted (2011) *The Annual Report of Her Majesty's Chief Inspector of Education, Children's Services and Skills 2010/11: Children's Social Care.* Available at: www.ofsted.gov.uk/resources/annualreport1011 (accessed 14 January 2013).

Ofsted (2012a) *Adoption Quality Assurance and Data Forms 2011–12: First Statistical Release.* Available at: http://www.ofsted.gov.uk/resources/adoption-quality-assurance-and-data-forms-2011-12-first-statistical-release (accessed 17 January 2013).

Ofsted (2012b) *Fostering Quality Assurance and Data Forms 2011–12 First Statistical Release.* Available at: http://www.ofsted.gov.uk/resources/fostering-quality-assurance-and-data-forms-2011-12-first-statistical-release (accessed 17 January 2013).

Ofsted (2012c) *Press Release: A State of the Nation Picture on Adoption.* Available at: http://www.ofsted.gov.uk/news/state-of-nation-picture-adoption?news=19995 (accessed 17 January 2013).

Ofsted (2012d) *The Impact of Virtual Schools on the Educational Progress of Looked After Children.* Available at: http://www.ofsted.gov.uk/resources/impact-of-virtual-schools-educational-progress-of-looked-after-children (accessed 17 January 2013).

Schofield G, Ward, E, Biggart, L, Scaife, V, Dodsworth, J, Larsson, B, Haynes, A and Stone, N (2012) *Looked After Children and Offending: Reducing Risk and Promoting Resilience.* Norwich: University of East Anglia. Available at: http://www.tactcare.org.uk/data/files/resources/52/lac_and_offending_reducing_risk_promoting_resilience_execsummary_080112.pdf (accessed 17 January 2013).

Social Exclusion Unit (2003) *A Better Education for Children in Care*: Social Exclusion Unit Report. London: Social Exclusion Unit. Available at: http://webarchive.nationalarchives.gov.uk/+/http://www.cabinetoffice.gov.uk/media/cabinetoffice/social_exclusion_task_force/assets/publications_1997_to_2006/abefcic_full%20report_1.pdf

Solihull Metropolitan Borough Council (2011) *Corporate Parenting Strategy, 2011 to 2015.* Available at: http://www.solihull.gov.uk/akssolihull/images/att33506.pdf (accessed 15 January 2013).

Stein, M (2008) *Young People Leaving Care.* Highlight Series; no.240. London: National Children's Bureau.

Tameside Metropolitan Borough Council (2012) *Corporate Parenting Strategy for Looked after Children 2012–2015.* Available at: www.tameside.gov.uk/lac/strategy/1215.pdf (accessed 15 January 2013).

Utting, W (1997) *People Like Us: The Report of the Review of the Safeguards for Children Living Away From Home.* London: Department of Health and Welsh Office.

Voice For the Child in Care (2004) *Start With the Child, Stay With the Child: A Blueprint for a Child-centred Approach to Children and Young People in Public Care.* London: Voice.

Wade, J, Biehal, N, Farrelly, N and Sinclair, I (2010) *Maltreated Children in the Looked After System: A Comparison of Outcomes for Those Who Go Home and Those Who Do Not.* Research Brief, DFE-RBX-10-06. London: Department for Education. Available at: http://php.york.ac.uk/inst/spru/pubs/1786/ (accessed 17 January 2013).

Ward, H, Soper, J, Holmes, L and Olsen, R (2004) *Looked After Children: Counting the Costs – Report on the Costs and Consequences of Different Types of Child Care Provision Study* (CCFR Evidence 7). Loughborough University: Centre for Child and Family Research.

Ward, H, Brown, R, Westlake, D and Munro, ER (2010) *Infants Suffering, or Likely to Suffer, Significant Harm: A Prospective Longitudinal Study.* London: Department for Education.

Available at: http://www.lboro.ac.uk/research/ccfr/Publications/DFE-RB053.pdf (accessed 17 January 2013).

Waterhouse, R, Clough, M and Le Flemming, M (2000) *Lost in Care: Report of the Tribunal of Inquiry into the Abuse of Children in Care in the Former County Council Areas of Gwynedd and Clwyd Since 1974.* Norwich: The Stationery Office.

Wokingham Borough Council (2012) *Corporate Parenting Board Strategy.* Available at: http://bit.ly/V3Cspl (accessed 22 January 2013).

Youth Justice Board (2012) *Implementation of the LASPO Act 2012: Key Stakeholder Information.* Available at: http://www.justice.gov.uk/youth-justice/courts-and-orders/legal-aid-sentencing-and-punishment-of-offenders-act-2012 (accessed 17 January 2013).